Risk and
Crisis Communication

Risk and Crisis Communication

Navigating the Tensions between Organizations and the Public

Edited by
Robert S. Littlefield and
Timothy L. Sellnow

LEXINGTON BOOKS
Lanham • Boulder • New York • London

Published by Lexington Books
An imprint of The Rowman & Littlefield Publishing Group, Inc.
4501 Forbes Boulevard, Suite 200, Lanham, Maryland 20706
www.rowman.com

Unit A, Whitacre Mews, 26-34 Stannary Street, London SE11 4AB

British Library Cataloguing in Publication Information Available

Library of Congress Cataloging-in-Publication Data Available

ISBN: 978-1-4985-1789-8 (cloth : alk. paper)
ISBN: 978-1-4985-1791-1 (pbk. : alk. paper)
ISBN: 978-1-4985-1790-4 (electronic)

∞™ The paper used in this publication meets the minimum requirements of
American National Standard for Information Sciences—Permanence of Paper
for Printed Library Materials, ANSI/NISO Z39.48-1992.

Printed in the United States of America

Contents

Contents

Introduction to the Dialectical Tensions of Risk and Crisis Communication

Robert S. Littlefield

Individuals, communities, and organizations face crises continually. A crisis is defined as, "a major occurrence with a potentially negative outcome affecting the organization, company, or industry, as well as its publics, products, services, or good name" (Fearn-Banks, 2011, p. 2). There are many different types of crises, including natural disasters (e.g., tornados, hurricanes, floods, and fires); crises that occur because of human error (e.g., airplanes crash landing due to miscalculation); and intentional crises (e.g., the economic adulteration of food products). We know a great deal about how these various crises develop. For example, Seeger, Sellnow, and Ulmer (2003) described how crises are signaled to the public in the pre-crisis stage when messages or signs foretell that something is going to happen; and when forces come together so that there is no longer a balance, a triggering event occurs to precipitate the crisis phase, forcing an organization to respond. Organizational learning occurs during the post-crisis phase as those affected by the crisis make sense of the crisis and its effects.

Many studies have explored how companies and organizations have dealt with crises (e.g., Benoit, 1995; Coombs, 1998; Covello et al., 2001; Weick, 1988); and scholars have identified these best practices after the fact as we have considered what has worked in this case or that case. Seeger (2006) defined best practices as, "a general set of standards, guidelines, norms, reference points or benchmarks that inform practice and are designed to improve performance" (p. 233); and others have identified when these best practices have occurred (see Borda & MacKallis, 2004; Covello, 1992; Heath, 2006; Reynolds & Seeger, 2005; Sellnow & Littlefield, 2005; Sellnow, Ulmer, Seeger, & Littlefield, 2009). In sum, best practices associated with strategic planning include planning for pre-crisis logistics, coordinating networks, and accepting uncertainty associated with crises; proactive strategies encompass forming partnerships, listening to public concerns, and being open and honest; and strategic responses involve being accessible to media, communicating compassion, and providing self-efficacy.

Situational Crisis Communication Theory (SCCT) provides a framework that helps explain why organizations respond to crises in particular (Coombs, 2004). After a crisis has occurred, an organization has to decide how it is going to respond. Invariably, successful companies who survive their crises use some or all of these best practices. We know that the best practices are organizational, and situated within the purview of the affected entity when it decides what should be done before a crisis occurs. But, we also know there are audience-focused best practices used when organizations are interacting with their stakeholders (e.g., people and the public). These best practices organize themselves at the intersection of the organization and audience, or intended audiences.

Best practices do not occur simultaneously within the span of a crisis. Rather, an interaction within a crisis context occurs depending upon the situation. Beauchamp and Littlefield (2011) supported this perspective with their study of the Maple Leaf Foods recall, demonstrating where the emphasis of the company changed over the course of the crisis. For example, when the crisis began, the company used multiple spokespeople when communicating with the public. However, once Maple Leaf Foods was linked with the contaminated meat products and public concern about the crisis grew, the CEO became the sole spokesperson and his empathy and concern for those affected by the contaminated products served to rebuild the image of the company in the minds of the affected publics.

While we know that there is an interaction, we often do not know how that interaction manifests itself. Within risk communication, no theory or explanation using our traditional models identifies the interplay of forces affecting the decision-making underway because it is not apologia, image restoration, diffusion, or excellence theory (Fearn-Banks, 2011) and it is not best practices functioning in a linear fashion. Rather, there is a dynamic that has not been explainable with theories in risk communication. Decision theory may provide the closest description of what is happening within an organization as management and other leaders are "counseling . . . to make the most effective decision" (Fearn-Banks, p. 19). However, even this perspective focuses on the ends or outcomes—the best decision—not the *hows* or means by which an organization arrives at that decision.

We have observed that, when best practices are being considered, there are certain tensions organizations respond to; and that is the focus of this book. These tensions are similar to those experienced between individuals when managing their interpersonal relationships. As such, we turned to a theory originating outside of the context of organizational or risk/crisis communication known as relational dialectics theory (RDT) (Baxter & Montgomery, 1996). There are three components to this interpersonal theory describing the tensions in a relationship: how much information should be shared, how much certainty versus uncertainty should be included in the message, and the timing of the message. We concluded that there might be some aspects of this theory that are useful as we explore risk or crisis situations. The result of our hunch is this book, providing a more robust explanation of RDT as exemplified through seven case studies of crisis situations, each focusing on one of the tensions. We conclude with a chapter synthesizing the case study findings and demonstrating that our approach provides a meaningful way to extend understanding of the micro-processes involved as organizations work through the dialectical tensions inherent in risk and crisis situations.

THE BASICS OF RELATIONAL DIALECTICS

So first, let us explain some of the key elements of RDT; where it comes from, and some of the most significant studies that have focused on how tensions work.[1] To begin, RDT is an interpretive theory used to explain how meanings are understood between individuals in a relationship (Baxter, 2006; Baxter & Montgomery, 1996). The theoretical framework of relational dialectics is based on a process whereby competing perspectives are engaged in a discursive struggle to arrive at a point of understanding in order to maintain the relationship. The original theory describes the tensions in an interpersonal relationship associated with connectedness and separateness, openness and closed-ness, and certainty and uncertainty. How individuals communicate about these tensions determines the nature of their relationship. In organizations, we suggest that decision-makers experience such a struggle as they interact to determine how to best create messages that will sustain their own position or reputation while continuing a positive relationship with their stakeholders or publics.

RDT provides a multidimensional approach to relationship building because it recognizes that competing perspectives need not be judged as good or bad, better or worse than the other. Rather, within the relationship, choices are viewed as multidimensional. For example, the competing needs of an individual to feel closeness with another person while maintaining some personal distance do not necessarily reflect positive or negative qualities. Yet, finding the right point between these needs results in tension. Similarly, within organizations, the need to be open with the public about what is happening in a crisis situation while controlling the release of information until its accuracy can be verified represents a form of tension.

An essential element of RDT in interpersonal relationships is its focus on multi-vocality (or contradiction) that only can be voiced through communication between the individuals involved (Baxter & Pittman, 2001). Thus, meaning comes through the expression of the competing voices comprising the contradiction (Baxter, Hirokawa, Lowe, Nathan, & Pearce, 2004). Within organizations experiencing crisis situations, this interaction may reflect competing positions on a wide range of issues facing the decision-makers. How successfully these organizational leaders construct their meaning will determine whether or not they can maintain a positive relationship with their publics. For example, the organization's prior history and crisis reputation may impact its ability to respond effectively in the present if the publics' expectations are at odds with what the organization says or intends to do.

In short, the utility of using RDT to explain the dynamics of the micro-processes at work in organizations as they experience the tensions associated with arriving at and disseminating risk and crisis messages warrants further investigation. This book provides an opportunity for crisis communicators and managers to consider how such tensions are manifested in their organizations when faced with risk and crisis situations.

THE IMPACT OF CULTURE

In addition to examining the dynamics of decision-making in the formation of risk and crisis messages, we have chosen to explore more comprehensively risk and crisis communication from the receivers' or publics' points of view. Most studies have focused on some kind of general public and not the cultural components of risk and crisis communication and how culture exacerbates or heightens the tensions inherent in the situation.

For a number of reasons, previous research has focused on top down, sender-oriented communication, evaluating the effectiveness of particular strategies used by spokespeople to repair their image or apologize (Coombs, 2005). This sender-focused research has excluded the receiver from the analysis other than to suggest that the target audience be considered when constructing the message. This culture-neutral, or what some would consider objective view of the publics, has been applied as standard practice for elite risk and crisis communicators.

In contrast, within the realm of health communication, Dutta (2007) identified culture-centered communication as a form of interaction involving the affected publics in the dialogue, empowering them to determine their concerns and letting them focus the way messages are presented to them, what they want to hear, and how they want to hear it. This approach gained traction and some research has reflected aspects of culture-centeredness (Aldoory & Van Dyke, 2006; Eisenman, Cordasco, Asch et al., 2006; Grunig, 1997). Others have shared Dutta's approach, emphasizing community-based participation in creating programs and responding to crises. Lasker and colleagues (2001a, 2001b, 2003) demonstrated the benefits of working together collaboratively with cultural and community groups to promote synergy and improved self-efficacy of the publics. So, we concluded that in crisis situations, when multiple publics are involved, knowing more about those publics and how they prefer to receive the information they need to mitigate or protect themselves from crisis is vital. Thus, we adopted a culture-centered approach.

A culture-centered approach in this risk context is very similar to what Dutta conceptualized; asking individuals, cultural groups, or vulnerable populations to consider how they would like to get information, how much information they need, the timing of the information's release, and who would be the most credible sources of information. Of course, in the acute phase of a crisis enacting a culture-centered approach is difficult because there is not enough time to reach out and ask, "Okay, we're having a crisis now. How do you want to get the information we have to present?" During the pre-crisis stage, however, relationships can and should be developed and in place so that when a crisis occurs, the infrastructure and knowledge is available to be able to communicate effectively. In short, an ongoing effort to establish an emphasis on culture can add notably to the effectiveness of the message.

Realistically, because people do not take advantage of opportunities to engage cultural groups in meaningful ways before a crisis occurs, they attempt to be culturally sensitive. In this regard, if they have sensitivity, they will understand that they may need to present the information in a variety of languages, use a variety of media, or may need to use spokespeople who may be perceived by the local community as credible; and they may need to do the things that are going to enhance the audiences' receptivity to the message. These approaches are culturally sensitive, rather than culture-centered because the sender is still making the decisions about what is presented, when, and by whom.

So we have these three different approaches—culture-neutral, culture-centered, and culturally sensitive—and they clearly indicate dimensions of risk and crisis communication that need to be adhered to so we do not miss contacting a group or working effectively with a group because we are not aware of the cultural dimensions at work in a particular context. To add robustness to the cases studies included in this book, we have included a cultural dimension in order to identify the cultural variables at play in each crisis, and suggest how these cultural elements may have influenced the kinds of tensions each organization faced. There may be some inherent tensions in a risk or crisis situation that are more directly affected than others by culture. Thus, while each of the chapters has a cultural aspect added to the analysis, the influence of culture may be more or less consequential based upon how the organization dealt with the cultural dimensions, if at all, in the decision-making process.

THE ORGANIZATION OF THE BOOK

The dialectical tensions occurring when an organization experiences a crisis primarily find their roots in the prerequisite conditions of relational maintenance calling for the use of best practices. For example, the best practices of meeting the needs of the media and being accessible produce the dialectical tensions of *timeliness* (When should the organization be releasing information about the crisis to the media and public?), *amount of information revealed* (How much information should the organization reveal to the media and public?), and *voice(s) in media* (How much control of the crisis response narrative can the organization maintain through one or more spokespeople?). The best practices of accepting uncertainty and ambiguity and collaborating and coordinating with credible sources points to the dialectical tension of *confidence of information revealed* (How certain is the organization about the information to be revealed to the public?). The *prioritization of interest* dialectical tension stems from the best practices of hearing and understanding the public's concerns and fostering partnerships with the public (Whose interest—the organization's or the public's—should be prioritized as the crisis is managed?). The best practices of pre-event planning and preparedness and viewing risk and crisis communication as an ongoing process lead to the dialectical tension identifying *level of responsibility for crisis* (How much responsibility should the organization take for causing the crisis?). Finally, the best practices of hearing and understanding public concerns, as well as being open, candid, and honest with the public produce the dialectical tension of *emotional connection* (How much of an emotional connection should the organization maintain with the public?) (See Table 1.)

Table I.1. Best Practices, Tensions, and Questions to Consider in Risk and Crisis Management

Best Practices	Tensions	Questions to Consider
Meeting the needs of the media Being accessible	Timeliness	When should the organization be releasing information about the crisis to the media and the public?
	Amount of information	How much information should the organization reveal to the media and the public?
	Control of the narrative	How much control of the crisis response narrative can the organization maintain through one or more spokespeople?
Accepting uncertainty and ambiguity Collaborating and coordinating with credible sources	Confidence in information	How certain is the organization about the information to be revealed to the public?
Hearing and understanding publics' concerns Fostering partnerships	Prioritization of interest	Whose interest—the organization's or the public's—should be prioritized as the crisis is managed?
Pre-event planning and preparedness Viewing risk and crisis communication as process	Level of responsibility	How much responsibility should the organization take for causing the crisis?
Hearing and understanding publics' concerns Being candid, open, and honest with the public	Emotional connection	How much of an emotional connection should the organization maintain with the public?

Each of the cases in this book examines one of the tensions. We have identified seven dialectical tension of risk and crisis communication.

Timeliness: Immediate vs. Delayed

The question of when the organization should comment about a risk or crisis situation is identified in the first case study focusing on the Peanut Corporation of America peanut butter recall in 2009. The tension stemmed from the question of whether PCA should have provided an immediate or delayed response to the contamination of produce stored in its warehouses. In this case, PCA delayed the timing of its communication, resulting in a negative response from the public and the ultimate bankruptcy of PCA.

Amount of Information: Open vs. Closed

The amount of information shared by an organization with the public shapes the tension identified in the case study of the Menu Foods pet food recall of 2007. This tension occurred because Menu Foods weighed the option of being open to disclosing information about the risk of eating the pet food with the affected publics. For Menu Foods, the decision to not disclose during the early stages of the crisis resulted in the publics' displeasure with the company, ultimately resulting in the collapse of Menu Foods.

Confidence in Information: Certainty vs. Uncertainty

The confidence of the organization about the information being disseminated to the public is the focus of this tension, as revealed in the case of the 2011 vegetable recall in Germany. In this case, early messages were proven inaccurate, thereby reducing credibility of entities sending the messages. The result was profound distrust in those entities. In this case, acknowledgment of uncertainty would have given authorities the time they needed to verify the information about the source of the contamination. The result of this crisis was the initiation of reforms regarding origin of produce.

Focus of Interest: Self-Serving vs. Other-Serving

This tension focuses on the extent to which an organization should look out for its own interests instead of the protection and benefit of others. We chose the Chinese San Lu milk recall of 2008 to demonstrate this tension. In this case, San Lu initially was self-serving in its actions but later became other-serving. However, the result was extreme for San Lu, in that the company went bankrupt and some of those convicted of contaminating the milk were put to death.

Level of Responsibility: Owning vs. Disowning

Every organization must consider the tension posed by the question, to what extent must we assume responsibility for a crisis? Owning, or taking responsibility, is a critical issue that often is mitigated by the law and liability concerns. The Del Bueno Queso Fresco recall of 2012 demonstrated the result of how Del Bueno's disowning of its responsibility for the contamination and its failure to correct the problems resulted in the Food and Drug Administration's shut down of the company's factory operations.

Control of the Narrative: One Voice vs. Multiple Voices

Determining how many voices should communicate about a crisis is an inherent tension in the decision-making process. We chose the Proposition 37 debate in California over the labeling of genetically engineered (GE) foods to demonstrate this tension because the multiple voices of those favoring the narrative of labeling of GE foods to protect the public from harm challenged the scientific narrative adhered to by the Food and Drug Administration (FDA) claiming there was no evidence that GE foods posed any threat to humans. The inability for the competing narratives to intersect demonstrated the tension the FDA and anti-labeling groups faced in attempting to retain control of their narratives and influencing the outcome of the referendum. In this case, Proposition 37 was defeated. However, the significant support for the pro-labeling narrative suggested that the FDA and anti-labeling forces may have been hampered by having too many voices conveying their message, rather than using a single, credible source to lead the campaign against Proposition 37.

Empathy with the Publics: Sensitivity vs. Insensitivity

Our final tension revolves around the question of how much empathy should the organization demonstrate about the crisis with the public? The case of the Wright County Egg and Hillsdale Farms Egg Recall of 2010 provides an example of how the lack of sensitivity as shown by the company's owners resulted in the company's struggling to regain their status in the market among people with the capacity to make other egg selection choices. In this case, Wright County Egg and Hillsdale Farms demonstrated a lack of sensitivity.

SUMMARY

The chaotic nature of crisis is such that decision-makers often make choices that reflect the dialectical tensions inherent in the process of dealing with the situation at hand. We know that decision-makers often make strategic choices as to how they will respond to a crisis situation. Unfortunately, little is known about how they arrive at those choices. This chapter has provided a brief introduction to an interpersonal theory describing the tensions involved in a relationship and shown the potential for its usefulness in helping managers and decision-makers to understand how to navigate the choices resulting from a risk or crisis situation. In addition, the seven case studies identified serve as illustrations of the interaction between the best practices and the tensions involved. In the next chapter, the need for cultural awareness and responsiveness is offered as an essential element for decision-makers to consider when deciding how to create messages and respond most effectively in crisis situations.

NOTE

1. Portions of this discussion of relational dialectics theory were drawn from an unpublished paper authored by Robert S. Littlefield, and his graduate research assistants Laura Farrell, Kimberly Beauchamp, and Shalindra Rathnasinghe. The paper, entitled, "Maintaining Relationships with the Public: Applications of Relational Dialectics Theory in Crisis Communication," was presented at the 2012 National Communication Association Convention held in Orlando, Florida.

REFERENCES

Aldoory, L., & Van Dyke, M. (2006). The roles of perceived "shared" involvement and information overload in understanding how audiences make meaning of news about bioterrorism. *Journalism and Mass Communication Quarterly, 83*(2), 346–361. Retrieved from www.proquest.umi.com

Baxter, L. A. (2006). Relational dialectics theory: Multivocal dialogues of family communication. In D. O. Braithwaite & L. A. Baxter (Eds.), *Engaging theories in family communication: Multiple perspectives* (pp. 130–145). Thousand Oaks, CA: Sage.

Baxter, L. A., & Montgomery, B. M. (1996). *Relating: Dialogues & dialectics*. New York: Guilford Press.

Baxter, L. A. & Pittman, G. (2001). Communicatively remembering turning points of relationship development. *Communication Reports, 14*, 1–18.

Baxter, L. A., Hirokawa, R., Lowe, J., Nathan, P., & Pearce, L. (2004). Dialogic voices in talk about drinking and pregnancy. *Journal of Applied Communication Research, 32*, 224–248.

Beauchamp, K. L., & Littlefield, R. S. (2011). The Maple Leaf Foods recall: Best practice interaction during a food-related crisis. *International Journal of Business Continuity and Risk Management 3*(1), 1–18.

Benoit, W. L. (1995). *Accounts, excuses and apologies*. Albany, NY: State University Press.

Borda, J. L., & Mackey-Kallis, S. (2004). A model for crisis management. In D. P. Millar & R. Heath (Eds.), *A rhetorical approach to crisis communication* (pp. 117–138). Mahwah, NJ: Lawrence Erlbaum Associates.

Coombs, W. T. (1998). An analytic framework for crisis situations: Better responses from a better understanding of the situation. *Journal of Public Relations Research, 10*(3), 177–191.

Coombs, W. T. (2004). Impact of past crises on current crisis communication: Insights from situational crisis communication theory. *Journal of Business Communication, 41*(3), 265–289. doi:10.1177/0021943604265607

Coombs, W. T. (2005). Crisis communication. In R. L. Heath (Ed.), *Encyclopedia of public relations* (Vol. 1, pp. 221–223). Thousand Oaks, CA: Sage.

Covello, V. T. (1992). Risk communication: An emerging area of health communication research. In S. A. Deetz (Ed.), *Communication Yearbook, 15* (pp. 359–373). Newbury Park, CA: Sage.

Covello, V., Peters, R., Wojtecki, J., & Hyde, R. (2001). Risk communication, the West Nile Virus epidemic, and bioterrorism: Responding to the communication challenges posed by the intentional or unintentional release of a pathogen in an urban setting. *Journal of Urban Health: Bulletin of the New York Academy of Medicine, 78*(2), 382–391.

Dutta, M. J. (2007). Communicating about culture and health: Theorizing culture-centered and cultural sensitive approaches. *Communication Theory, 17*(3), 304–328.

Eisenman, D. P., Cordasco, K. M., Asch, S., Golden, J. F., & Glik, D. (2006). Disaster planning and risk communication with vulnerable communities: Lessons from Hurricane Katrina. *American Journal of Public Health, 97*(S1), 109–115. Retrieved from http://www.proquest.umi.com

Fearn-Banks, K. (2011). *Crisis communications: A casebook approach* (4th ed.). New York: Routledge.

Grunig, J. E. (1997). A situational theory of publics: Conceptual history, recent challenges and new research. In D. Moss, T. MacManus, & D. Vercic (Eds.), *Public relations research: An international perspective* (pp. 3–48). London: International Thomson Business Press.

Heath, R. (2006). Best practices in crisis communication: Evolution of practice through research. *Journal of Applied Communication Research, 34*(3), 245–248.

Lasker, R. D., & Weiss, E. S. (2003). Broadening participation in community problem solving: A multidisciplinary model to support collaborative practice and research. *Journal of Urban Health: Bulletin of the New York Academy of Medicine, 80*(1), 14–47.

Lasker, R. D., Weiss, E. S., & Miller, R. (2001a). Partnership synergy: A practical framework for studying and strengthening the collaborative advantage. *The Milbank Quarterly, 9*(2), 179–205.

Lasker, R. D., Weiss, E. S., & Miller, R. (2001b). Promoting collaborations that improve health. *Education for Health, 14*(2), 163–172.

Reynolds, B., & Seeger, M. W. (2005). Crisis and emergency risk communication as an integrative model. *Journal of Health Communication, 10*(1), 43–55.

Seeger, M. W. (2006). Best practices in crisis communication: An expert panel process. *Journal of Applied Communication Research, 34*(3), 232–244.

Seeger, M. W., Sellnow, T. L., & Ulmer, R. R. (2003). *Communication and organizational crises.* Westport, CN: Praeger.

Sellnow, T. L., & Littlefield, R. S. (Eds.). (2005). *Case studies in crisis communication: Lessons learned about protecting America's food supply.* Fargo, ND: North Dakota Institute for Regional Studies.

Sellnow, T. L., Ulmer, R. R., Seeger, M. W., & Littlefield, R. S. (2009). *Effective risk communication: A message-centered approach.* New York: Springer.
Weick, K. E. (1988). Enacting sensemaking in crisis situations. *Journal of Management Studies, 25*(4), 305–317.

Chapter One

Adding the Focus on Culture as a Best Practice

Robert S. Littlefield

For nearly a decade, some practitioners and scholars studying risk and crisis communication have been arguing that cultural perspectives must be included among the best practices and taken into consideration when developing and presenting risk and crisis messages to different publics (Littlefield, 2013; Sellnow, Johnson, Ulmer et al., 2008; Sellnow, Ulmer, Seeger, & Littlefield, 2009). This call for cultural consideration came in response to the fact that for quite some time, most crisis decision-makers were not considering cultural variables in their management of crisis situations because they focused mostly on the effects of the crisis. Typically, the nature of research on the subject of risk and crisis has been to examine what happened during the pre-crisis, crisis, and post-crisis phases and then interpret and evaluate how an organization or entity responded (see Barton, 1993; Benoit, 1995, 1997; Covello, 2003; Heath, 1997; Lindell & Perry, 2004; Weick, 1988).

CULTURAL APPROACHES TO MESSAGE DEVELOPMENT

Occasionally, some research about the effects of a crisis emerged from the field as well as how cultural groups were adversely affected by particular crises. For example, some groups may have been particularly vulnerable to a crisis because of their economic status, level of education, or particular location of residence (Spence, Lachlan, & Griffin, 2007). What we don't know is how cultural considerations influenced decision-makers as they responded through their communication during the crisis situation. At worst, decision-makers may have taken what they considered to be an objective, or culture-neutral point of view, with their messages making no particular mention of different cultural groups within the general context. At best, decision-makers may have included members of particular cultural publics to be part of their decision-making process in shaping the risk and crisis messages. If cultural representatives were not included in the process, the organization may still have attempted to be culturally sensitive in the content and delivery of its risk and crisis messages based upon its best judgment about how to gain compliance to its requests for particular behavior.

Culture-Neutral Approach

To begin, most crafters of risk and crisis messages rely on a process that convenes the most informed people within an organization and provides them with all of the available information about the crisis situation. These people then go on to prepare a message that they believe any *reasonable* person should understand. Typically, this message is fact-based, and involves scientific explanations. Often, the message is released specifically because it is objective; as objectivity in the scientific communication is valued (e.g., researchers test for validity of measurement and reliability of data to produce an objective conclusion).

Coming from this perspective, organizational spokespeople presenting objective risk or crisis messages believe that such messages will be viewed positively by those who receive them because they are not subject to interpretation; facts are perceived as facts. These objective messages are what we identify as culture-neutral because they do not take culture into account. Those presenting culture-neutral messages may consider the inclusion of culture in the construction of a risk or crisis message as revealing an inherent subjectivity; thereby reducing the scientific validity and/or reliability of the message. Because the content of the message would be viewed as biased or subjective, it would not be acceptable from an intelligent, objective, scientific perspective.

Culturally Sensitive Approach

The second approach an organization might use involves being culturally sensitive. A number of advertising studies determined that people respond positively to such particularly sensitive messages (Fink, 1986; Leanna, Ahlbrant, & Murrell, 1992; Leitch & Neilson, 1997; McMahan, Witte, & Meyer, 1998). For example, if a decision-maker is developing a message for an African American group, the decision to use an African American spokesperson may be made to enhance the receptivity of the African American audience to the message. Or, a decision-maker may determine that the intended audience members cannot read a message in English; therefore, a version in Spanish is made available. While it may be that those who speak Spanish might not be able to read it, the act of providing a version in Spanish reflects the decision of the sender to present a message in a most desirable manner.

Decision-makers are in the position to choose message strategies that they think will be effective. While they may have some indication that a particular culturally sensitive approach might work, a great deal of subjective guess-work is involved. The message strategy may work with the intended audience or it may not.

Culture-Centered Approach

Finally, the third option for an organization developing a message strategy may be to have a local team or group that has connections with the various communities or publics where the message is going to be sent and involve them in the process of message building and transmission; actually making representatives of the different publics part of the team. This community-based approach has been widely used in health campaigns and has utility in other contexts (Lasker & Weiss, 2003; Lasker, Weiss, & Miller, 2001), such as risk and crisis situations. This can be enacted by having co-researchers or co-participants who are familiar with the local culture working with the decision-makers and crafting the message so it is distributed effectively; or if such relationship building has been enacted previously during the pre-crisis stage, a network/infrastructure may already be in place and the risk or crisis message can be developed and transmitted immediately into a form that is acceptable to the local community.

Decision-makers are left with these three approaches as they prepare their risk or crisis messages, and attention to cultural considerations becomes a dimension of a message's effectiveness. Realistically, the more in line the message is with how the local group prefers to receive the information, the more likely the intended publics are going to respond in ways that the sender intends (Littlefield, Beauchamp, Lane et al., 2014). Thus, culture should be a part of the best practices because in those situations where communication is tailored with cultural considerations in mind (e.g., receiving information in a way that would be effective with a group) the more likely decision-makers are going to be able to get the responses they want. When cultural considerations are not taken into account for the local publics, the recipients of the messages are not likely to respond as desired and can be adversely affected. The Hurricane Katrina crisis stands as an example where the risk and crisis messages did not take culture into consideration and the result for the local public produced horrific consequences in New Orleans (Spence et al., 2007).

Culture as a Best Practice

So, we know that considering culture in message design is helpful; but why is it a best practice? Where does it fit in the realm of risk and crisis communication? Quite simply, including cultural considerations as part of the best practices has given weight to the argument that the decision-maker has made the effort to consider the different groups or publics being addressed and that the resulting message is either culturally sensitive or culture-centered, depending upon the advance work completed prior to the crisis context.

Some of the questions to consider when cultural issues are included in message development and transmission might include: What are the cultural characteristics of the group being addressed and how can the intended message best be conveyed in order to gain the greatest compliance from the intended audience?

CULTURAL DIMENSIONS: AFFECTING RECEPTIVITY OF MESSAGES

We know that context exists, and every culture exists in a context. Thus, the first question for decision-makers might be: "What are the languages or code systems being used by the people in a particular cultural context?" Using a common code between the sender and the receiver of a risk or crisis message should be a priority. This includes both the language used and the mode for the transmission of the message. Another question addresses the issue of knowing and accepting the normative beliefs and values of the cultural groups being addressed: "What do they think?" "How do they feel?" and "What do they believe about things that affect them?" And more important than simply knowing, decision-makers must be able to accept the fact that they may not accept for themselves the beliefs and values of those receiving the messages. Instead, they must either find a way to help the receivers to look at the situation differently, or the decision-makers must develop communication strategies that focus on the issues believed to be true or important to the cultural groups. Local, cultural agents can help the decision-makers to convey the relevance and importance of the messages being transmitted.

A third aspect of culture must identify the perceived relationship and intent between the sender of the risk and crisis message and those who will receive the message. Perception is key and many cultural groups are sensitive to this issue due to a history of interaction between elites who appeared to have the interests of the cultural group in mind but in actuality were more interested in how they could benefit personally (see Caldwell, Davis, DeBois et al., 2005; Chino & DeBruyn, 2006; Cochan, Marshall, Garcia-Downing et al., 2008). Thus, the question for decision-makers becomes: "What is the nature of the intent toward the group receiving the message?" "Is your purpose to help them, hurt them, or ignore them?"

Most competent risk and crisis communicators believe that a helping intent is the basis for their messages. However, if the message violates a cultural norm or practice of the intended receiver, the sender might be perceived as wanting to hurt or injure the group. The recipient of the message is the one who determines perception of intent, not the sender. Having a local, cultural agent to assist may provide a way for communicators to reveal the true intent of their risk and crisis messages (Littlefield & Thweatt, 2004).

Finally, understanding the worldview of the intended audience is essential. Because there are different worldviews, risk and crisis messages are often considered variously by different cultural groups. Three worldviews that influence message receptivity include: the worldview of dominance; the worldview of equality or balance; and the worldview of subjugation. If the worldview is one of subjugation and characterized as fatalistic (e.g., bad things are going to happen and there is nothing I can do about it), it is hard for risk and crisis communicators to be successful with a message of self-efficacy. In contrast, self-efficacy would be very important to people who think that they can control what happens to them.

There are strategies that have utility for those attempting to gain compliance with people having different worldviews. For example, when some do not think they have any control over what happens to them, it may be necessary for the sender of the message to identify a different reason to motivate the recipient to respond as directed. In this case, instead of doing something to save themselves, the messages may direct people to do something to save their families or community. We have found that while an individual may be willing to be subjugated personally to the negative effects of a crisis, that individual may be unwilling to stand by and not do something to protect a family member or someone else relying on their protection (e.g., "You need to do this because you are going to have to watch out for your family and take care of them").

An understanding of different cultural worldviews becomes a critical part of creating the risk or crisis message; and, if these matters are not taken into account, the sender of the message is not going to be perceived as an effective communicator no matter what else is done. Without taking cultural aspects into consideration, the message is simply not going to come across as intended. And so, including the process of considering cultural variables (code systems, belief structures, perceptions of intent, and worldview) as a part of the best practices of risk and crisis communication is essential.

If the message makers are sensitive to cultural dimensions of communica
tion, they will be able to focus the message better to fit whatever level of ethnocentricity the person is experiencing. By way of explanation of ethnocentricity,
the closer we are to our own perspectives, the more motivated we tend to be
when responding. The term spheres of ethnocentricity (Littlefield & Cowden,
2006) and the idea of concentric rings is not new in terms of understanding
how people focus their attention (Dozier, Grunig, & Grunig, 1995; Lundgren
& McMakin, 2009).

However, in the area of risk and crisis communication, the concept of
spheres of ethnocentricity is novel and extends our understanding. Spheres
of ethnocentricity account for the fact that people often respond best to
messages that are focused on them. Individuals are the center of their uni-
verse; and as long as they are reached where they are at in the spheres, they
will be more likely to respond as directed. For example, people may be
concerned about their families, so understanding that sphere is necessary;
or their neighborhood, town, community, region, or country. Understanding that people are at different places in the spheres is another dimension
of the cultural aspects of risk and crisis communication. Some cultures are
more collectivistic, so their circles would extend further; others are more
individualistic and so they believe that, "it's more about me and my immediate family and what I'm doing." Messages need to focus on the level
of attention a cultural group may have in order for the intended group to
respond as intended.

Thus far, we have provided a general discussion about previous knowledge of crisis and the absence of culture. While there have been some calls
for more attention to cultural aspects in terms of how we address it in crisis,
scholars and practitioners really have not considered how or why culture
should be included as a best practice. We now move to a more specific focus
on how consideration of culture has been integrated into our analysis of particular risk and crisis situations.

Consideration of Culture as a Best Practice

This chapter has set up our contention that consideration of the cultural context of a situation should be included as a best practice; and how attention to
the cultural dimensions may in fact affect the tensions and decisions that are
made by organizations or decision-makers in the crisis situations. For each of
the case studies included this book, a cultural dimension has been included
to provide some context and to demonstrate that it could be a factor in ways
that may or may not have been anticipated (see Table 1.1).

Table 1.1.   Case, Tension, and Particular Cultural Variable(s) Influencing Message Reception

Case	Tension	Cultural Variable(s)
PCA	Timeliness	Perceived Relationship and Intent Worldview
Menu Foods	Amount of Information	Perceived Relationship and Intent Knowing and Accepting Normative Beliefs and Values Worldview
European Vegetables	Confidence in Information	Perceived Relationship and Intent Worldview
Sanlu Milk	Focus of Interest	Perceived Relationship and Intent Knowing and Accepting Normative Beliefs and Values
Del Bueno Fresco	Level of Responsibility	Perceived Relationship and Intent Knowing and Accepting Normative Beliefs and Values Worldview
California Proposition 37	Control of Narrative	Perceived Relationship and Intent Worldview
Wright County/ Hillsdale Farms Eggs	Emotional Connection	Code System Perceived Relationship and Intent Knowing and Accepting Normative Beliefs and Values

Peanut Corporation of America: Timeliness

The cultural dimensions examined with regard to the Peanut Corporation of America (PCA) involved perceived relationship and intent, and worldview. Because children and individuals rely on peanut butter as a trusted food (worldview), the fact that PCA distributed contaminated products and did not release information in a timely manner to schools and care facilities reflected a hurting intent (perceived relationship and intent) on the part of PCA.

Menu Foods: Amount of Information

In the case of Menu Foods, this was a domestic crisis for the United States market with international cultural implications (worldview). Chinese suppliers of ingredients used in the preparation of pet food were found to be harmful (perceived relationship and intent). The failure of Menu Foods to provide all of the information to pet owners resulted in the deaths of thousands of animals that were considered to be members of their owners' families (knowing and accepting normative beliefs and values).

European Vegetables:
Confidence in Information

This crisis began as a domestic crisis for Germany that took on international implications as additional information revealed inaccuracies in previous reports. Germany has one of the strongest European economies and the vegetable crisis had less impact upon German citizens than it ultimately did on poorer European Union countries that became more culpable as the crisis implications spread across the continent (worldview). Because the early information being released about the crisis was inaccurate, relationships on multiple levels were strained (perceived relationship and intent).

Sanlu Milk: Focus of Interest

The Sanlu Milk crisis occurred as the world was introduced to the Chinese culture through the eyes of the 2008 Olympic Games being staged in Beijing. Having a public relations crisis of this kind stemming from the perceived self-interest of a company out to make a profit became a major face-saving issue for Sanlu from both governmental and consumer perspectives (knowing and accepting normative beliefs and values). Because those most affected by this crisis were infants, the intent of Sanlu was perceived as one of harming (perceived relationship and intent). Similarly, because the additive was viewed as a deceptive way to increase the cost of the product to the consumer, a hurtful intent was perceived.

Del Bueno Fresco Cheese: Level of Responsibility

In the case of Del Bueno Fresco, a small, minority-based company was cited as having sold contaminated cheese within the dominant cultural community (worldview). The cheese product was a cultural food prepared in a manner consistent with norms in Mexico (knowing and accepting normative beliefs and values). While the company owners acknowledged the problem, without the resources to make the necessary safety changes in their processing of the cheese, they continued to produce contaminated products that made the public sick (perceived relationship and intent). The company was finally forced out of business by governmental agencies.

Proposition 37 Labeling of Genetically Engineered Food: Control of the Narrative

The California proposition involving the labeling of genetically engineered (GE) food resulted from a challenge to the dominant scientific narrative by members of the public whose counter narrative suggested that the absence of a label implied a cover-up and the potential for harms resulting from the consumption of GE food. This tension resulted from the perceptions of the pro-labeling publics that the intent of those who promoted the narrative supporting GE foods was to put consumers at risk by withholding information. While this was a domestic, state issue, there were international implications as GE food is widespread around the globe. The cultural groups included those who accepted the scientific narrative and those who subscribed to the worldview narrative that humans should not dominate nature by genetically engineering food products.

Wright County/Hillsdale Farm Eggs: Emotional Connection

When eggs from two major producers were found to be contaminated, Wright County and Hillsdale Farm Eggs communicated with the consumers in ways that were not understandable (code systems, knowing and accepting norma-tive beliefs and values) and reflected a general insensitivity to the plight of those who had been affected (perceived relationship and intent). The lack of understanding regarding the health literacy of the consumers demonstrated a lack of empathy and emotional connection with the publics.

APPLICATIONS OF CULTURAL CONSIDERATIONS IN RISK AND CRISIS SITUATIONS

How do we use this best practice of considering culture in risk and crisis situations? Where is this focused? In actuality, attention to cultural considerations may be bidirectional: focused on both the organization and audience. Clearly, being aware of cultural dimensions should be something that organizations strive to accomplish. So, awareness of culture clearly has an organizational focus. Decision-makers need to make this practice a legitimate part, not just a token, of organizational practice. Decision-makers should make cultural considerations a part of all of the risk and crisis discussions in order to take into account the code systems, normative beliefs and values, perceptions of relationships and intent, and worldview. This makes cultural considerations distinct from the other best practices and pervasive across all discussions.

Including cultural considerations in the creation and transmission of mes-sages is also audience focused because, if decision-makers are attentive to the local community being addressed, they will have more credibility. Studies show that if the local people perceive that their interests are being addressed or considered, they are more appreciative, interested, and likely to respond as instructed (Littlefield, Cowden, & Hueston, 2007). Hence, credibility is one way that the best practice of considering culture is audience-centered; and it may increase the likelihood that the people who should benefit from paying attention to the message will do so. Focusing on the different audiences affected by a risk or crisis situation might also increase the visibility of vulnerable people who might not otherwise be considered during a crisis situation.

In the following chapters, seven tensions experienced by decision-makers as they managed risk or crisis situations are revealed. As you examine these case studies, consider the impact of culture on the particular tensions identified. With a more robust understanding of the situation, consider potential strategies that might provide for more effective message construction and transmission in risk and crisis situations.

REFERENCES

Barton, L. (1993). *Crisis in organizations: Managing communication in the heat of chaos.* Cincinnati, OH: South-Western.

Benoit, W. L. (1995a). *Accounts, excuses and apologies.* Albany, NY: State University Press.

Benoit, W. L. (1997). Image restoration discourse and crisis communication. *Public Relations Review, 23,* 177–186.

Caldwell, J. Y., Davis, J. D., DuBois, B., Echo-Hawk, H., Erickson, J. S., Goins, R. T., et al. (2005). Culturally competent research with American Indians and Alaska natives: Findings and recommendations of the First Symposium of the Work Group on American Indian Research and Program Evaluation Methodology. *American Indian and Alaska Native Mental Health Research: The Journal of the National Center, 12*(1), 1–21. Retrieved 27 March 2013 from http://www.ebscohost.com

Chino, M., & DeBruyn, L. (2006). Building true capacity: Indigenous models for indigenous communities. *American Journal of Public Health, 96*(4), 596–599. Retrieved 27 March 2013 from http://www.ebscohost.com

Cochran, P. A., Marshall, C. A., Garcia-Downing, C., Kendall, E., Cook, D., McCubbin, L. et al. (2008). Indigenous ways of knowing: Implications for participatory research and community. *American Journal of Public Health, 98*(1), 22–27. Retrieved 27 March 2013 from http://web.ebscohost.com

Covello, V. T. (2003). Best practices in public health risk and crisis communication. *Journal of Health Communication Research, 8,* 5–8.

Dozier, D. M., Grunig, L. A., & Grunig, J. E. (1995). *Manager's guide to excellence in public relations and communication management.* Mahwah, NJ: Lawrence Erlbaum.

Fink, S. (1986). Crisis management: Planning for the inevitable. New York: American Management Association.

Heath, R. L. (1997). *Strategic issues management: Organizations and public policy challenges.* Thousand Oaks, CA: Sage.

Lasker, R. D., & Weiss, E. S. (2003). Broadening participation in community problem solving: A multidisciplinary model to support collaborative practice and research. *Journal of Urban Health, 80*(1), 14–47.

Lasker, R. D., Weiss, E. S., & Miller, R. (2001). Partnership synergy: A practical framework for studying and strengthening the collaborative advantage. *The Milbank Quarterly, 79*(2), 179–205.

Leanna, C. E., Ahlbrant, R. S., & Murrell, A. J. (1992). The effects of employee involvement programs on unionized workers' attitudes, perceptions, and preferences in decision making. *The Academy of Management Journal, 4,* 581–592.

Leitch, S., & Neilson, D. (1997). Reframing public relations: New directions for theory and practice. *Australian Journal of Communication 24*(2), 17–32.

Lindell, M. K., & Perry, R. W. (2004). *Communicating environmental risk in multiethnic communities.* Thousand Oaks, CA: Sage.

Littlefield, R. S. (2013). Communicating risk and crisis communication to multiple publics. In A. J. DuBrin (Ed.), *Crisis leadership in organizations* (pp. 231–251). Northampton, MA: Edward Elgar Publishing Ltd.

Littlefield, R. S., Beauchamp, K., Lane, D., Sellnow, D. D., Sellnow, T. L., Venette, S., Wilson, B. (2014). Instructional crisis communication: Connecting ethnicity and sex in the assessment of receiver-oriented message effectiveness. *Journal of Management and Strategy,* 5(3), doi: 10.5430/jms.v5n3p

Littlefield, R. S., & Cowden, K. (2006, November 17). Rethinking the single spokesperson model. Paper presented to the Public Relations Division of the National Communication Association, San Antonio, TX.

Littlefield, R. S., Cowden, K., & Hueston, W. (2007). *Crisis and risk communication: 10 tips for public health professionals communicating with Native and New Americans.* Fargo, ND: Institute for Regional Studies.

Littlefield, R. S., & Thweatt, T. S. (2004). The use of cultural agents as data collectors in Bosnian, Roma, Sudanese, and Somali groups. *Journal of Intercultural Communication Research, 33*(2), 77–87.

Lundgren, R. E., & McMakin, A. H. (2009). *Risk communication: A handbook for communicating environmental, safety, and health risks.* Hoboken, NJ: Wiley.

McMahan, S., Witte, K., & Meyer, J. (1998). The perception of risk messages regarding electromagnetic fields: Extending the extended parallel process model to an unknown risk. *Health Communication, 10,* 247–260.

Sellnow, T. L., Ulmer, R. R., Seeger, M. W., & Littlefield, R. S. (2009). *Effective risk communication: A message-centered approach.* New York: Springer.

Sellnow, T. L., Johnson, S., Ulmer, R. R., Seeger, M. W., Novak, J. M., Littlefield, R. S., & Venette, S. J. (2008). Confounding issues for implementing best practices in risk communication. White Paper. Minneapolis, MN: National Center for Food Protection and Defense.

Spence, P. R., Lachlan, K. A., & Griffin, D. R. (2007). Crisis communication, race, and natural disasters. *Journal of Black Studies, 37*(4), 539–554.

Weick, K. E. (1988). Enacting sensemaking in crisis situations. *Journal of Management Studies, 25*(4), 305–317.

Chapter Two

The Tension of Timeliness

*How Timing Proved Costly for
Peanut Corporation of America*

Shalindra Rathnasinghe and Robert S. Littlefield

Over the years, peanut butter has become a staple food not only for Americans, but for people from different cultures who make the United States their home. In America, the sale of peanut butter is a 900 million dollar a year operation (Severson, 2009). Due to its high concentration of protein and affordability, peanut butter especially has become a major food choice among the poor. In addition, peanut butter is widely offered in public schools, on military bases, and in nursing homes as a primary food source; and millions of people regularly buy cereals, cookies, and candy with peanut butter as an ingredient. Peanut butter's widespread popularity, with the exception of those who have a peanut allergy, makes finding households that do not have at least one peanut butter product relatively rare.

In the midst of this popularity, tragedy struck in 2009 when the peanut butter industry experienced a major salmonella contamination. Over a period of several months, people became ill after consuming peanut products; and the crisis worsened when deaths were reported by the media. This contamination was especially unfortunate for many of those who depended upon peanut butter (e.g., children, the elderly, and those with compromised immune systems). Stories emerged of the harmful circumstances experienced by the victims (Harris, 2009; Layton, 2009). As a result of this contamination, nine lives were lost and many more harmed by the adverse effects of eating the peanut butter products. The contamination not only resulted in loss of lives but a loss of revenue for many companies and stores and hardship for the people who depended on it.

The outbreak was eventually linked to Peanut Corporation of America (PCA), a peanut processing company founded in 1977, and based in Lynchburg, Virginia (Chapman & Newkirk, 2009). Stewart Parnell, the owner of PCA, ran the peanut company from a converted garage behind his house

(Layton & Miroff, 2009) while the company operated processing facilities in Blakely, Georgia; Suffolk, Virginia; and Plainview, Texas. Parnell found success by operating a low-cost business that relied on the cheapest peanuts available and using minimum wage labor and a bare-bones front office (Layton & Miroff, 2009). His family business supplied peanuts, peanut butter, peanut meal, and peanut paste to schools and nursing homes; to well-known companies such as Kellogg, Sara Lee, and Little Debbie; and to food processors that used the peanut products in a wide range of food items. Furthermore, the U.S. federal government bought products including PCA's ingredients for at-risk school children, disaster victims, and military troops; and Parnell even advised the Department of Agriculture on peanut quality. In all, PCA manufactured nearly 2.5 percent of the nation's processed peanuts (Chapman & Newkirk, 2009).

The investigation into PCA revealed the malicious actions of its owner, Stewart Parnell. E-mails and memos obtained by investigators found that Parnell shipped contaminated ingredients to customers with a homemade certificate that falsely indicated their purity (Layton, 2009). Evidence revealed that while the samples taken from the plant on August 11, 2008, tested positive for salmonella, Parnell sent samples to another laboratory where they tested negative for salmonella. As a result, instead of destroying what may have been tainted products, Parnell instructed his staff to ship them: "Okay, let's turn them loose then," wrote Parnell to the plant manager (Layton, 2009, p. A02). As was evident in the case of Peanut Corporation America, the organization did not take precautions, and as a result, threatened its stakeholder companies and the lives of many people.

The PCA crisis is complex because the company primarily functioned as an ingredient supplier to other manufacturers, but it also sold products directly to consumers. The latter role was only revealed after an investigation into its business practices. This combination of roles complicated perceptions from both manufacturers and the public regarding levels of timeliness. On the one hand, PCA failed to respond to allegations made by distributors; on the other, the company was completely silent on the products directly sold to consumers. PCA's failure to be timely in its revelations regarding tainted peanuts resulted in extending the crisis and its effects.

CULTURAL CONTEXT

Peanut butter is an iconic food that many Americans prefer. Today, peanut butter is used in many commercial products, such as confections, cereals, and snack foods. Compared to other high protein foods, peanut butter is very affordable. The most expensive all-natural organic varieties are cheaper per serving than most cuts of meat (Knerl, 2007). This is one of the reasons why subsidized food programs regularly include peanut butter as a staple for the average diet (Knerl, 2007). Thus, it was not surprising that the contamination's effects were experienced among the poor, both young and the old. Unfortunately, many of the victims and fatalities were among the economically disadvantaged and elderly population.

The data revealed many people who were sickened by the contaminated products were depending on subsidized programs. The federal government itself bought from PCA and supplied it to poor schoolchildren, disaster victims, and military troops. PCA products also were sent to nursing homes, where in the case of two-time cancer survivor Shirley Almer, her death was directly tied to the consumption of the tainted peanut butter (Layton, 2009). Another victim was Clifford Tousignant, a Korean War veteran and recipient of three Purple Heart medals, who died from eating the peanut butter (Andrews, 2009).

Children were another vulnerable group affected by the contaminated peanut butter. As early as the 1920s, with the invention of sliced bread, it became easier for children to make their own peanut butter sandwiches without the need to handle sharp knives ("Peanut butter," 2012). Soon, peanut butter sandwiches became one of the top children's meals in America. When such a trusted product contributes to the illness of children, as was the case with Christopher Meunier, the outrage of the public can become more extreme (Harris, 2009). Because of the vulnerability of those who relied on peanut butter and peanut butter products, the timeliness of informing these groups about the potential risks was even more critical.

THEORETICAL FRAMEWORK

Relational dialectics theory (RDT) offers a conceptual framework to explore dialectical tensions that emerge within crisis situations and place the focus on organizational relationships (Baxter & Montgomery, 1996). RDT can be used to explore the decision-making processes associated with constructing and disseminating messages in crisis situations. Littlefield, Farrell, Beauchamp, and Rathnasinghe (2012) identified seven dialectical tensions drawn from best practices literature, and used them to demonstrate the utility of RDT in better understanding the issues organizations face when deciding how to maintain relationships with the public. The best practices of meeting the needs of the media and being accessible produced the dialectical tensions of *timeliness*.

The tension of timeliness involves the continuum with two opposing points: immediate and delayed (Littlefield et al., 2012). A timely response consists of publicizing information at appropriate times because stakeholders, in particular, demand information and answers during a crisis (Coombs, 1999). Seeger (2006) noted that during a crisis the public should be told what is happening, and the organization managing the crisis should share this information in a timely manner.

The sense of urgency associated with a crisis is further intensified by the arrival of new technologies, such as social media, that can broadcast information at a rapid pace (Lee, 2005). The introduction of social media can make an event more unpredictable, impose significant threats on information management, and affect normal organizational functioning (Lee, 2005). Communicating candidly with the media in a timely and efficient fashion is one of the characteristics that differentiate those who are treated fairly and forthrightly by the media and those who have difficulties with both the crisis and the media's coverage (Barton, 1991). The urgency, threats, surprises, and public doubts regarding a corporation's loss of control that often accompanies a crisis can be eased by a timely response (Coombs, 1999). Timely messages and statements have been found to be key factors that can foster stakeholder satisfaction and trust (Augustine, 1995; Strong, Ringer, & Taylor, 2001). However, when a company fails to communicate during a crisis, the relationship with its stakeholders can deteriorate (Martinelli & Briggs, 1998).

TIMELINE

As the crisis unraveled, PCA failed to be timely in its responses and actions. When the stakeholders demanded more information PCA became even more reticent. PCA's strategy of issuing ambiguous and delayed responses to officials, distributors, and customers limited its ability to stay in business. In the end, PCA actions led the company into bankruptcy (see Table 2.1).

RESEARCH QUESTIONS

In order to understand the dialectical tension of timeliness this chapter explores the pre-crisis, crisis, and post-crisis actions taken by PCA and addresses the following questions:

RQ #1:   How did PCA navigate the dialectical tension of timeliness when dealing with the *Salmonella* crisis?

RQ #2:   How did the cultural context affect the ability of PCA to resolve the crisis?

Table 2.1.   Crisis Timeline for Peanut Butter Recall

PRE-CRISIS PHASE

Sept. 8, 2008	First reports surfaced of illnesses connected to *Salmonella*, according to CDC.
Nov. 25, 2008	CDC, began an epidemiological assessment of a cluster of *Salmonella* cases reported from twelve different states.
Dec. 3, 2008– Jan. 6, 2009	FDA and CDC coordinated investigation into the source of contamination in peanut products linked to an outbreak of *Salmonella Typhimurium*.
Dec. 21, 2008	Victim died in Brainerd, Minn.
Jan. 7, 2009	CDC reported 388 people infected with *Salmonella Typhimurium* in forty-two states.
Jan. 8, 2009	FDA initiated inspection and collected samples at peanut butter distributor, King Nut; FDA determined that the manufacturer of King Nut brand peanut butter was PCA in Blakely, Georgia.

CRISIS PHASE

Jan. 9, 2009	FDA initiated inspection and sampled collections over the course of fourteen days with six investigators onsite at PCA's Blakely facility; PCA ceased production and shipment of peanut paste and peanut butter.
Jan. 10, 2009	King Nut announced a recall of peanut butter distributed under the King Nut and Parnell's Pride labels.
Jan. 12, 2009	FDA collaborated with CDC, USDA, and state public health officials to investigate a multi-state outbreak of infections due to *Salmonella Typhimurium*.
Jan. 13, 2009	PCA announced a voluntary recall of twenty-one specific lots of peanut butter and peanut paste produced at its Blakely facility on or after July 1, 2008.
Jan. 16, 2009	PCA expanded its recall to include all peanut butter produced on or after Aug. 8, 2008, and all peanut paste produced on or after Sept. 26, 2008.
Jan. 17, 2009	FDA announced that it notified PCA that product samples from its Blakely facility had been tested and found positive for *Salmonella* by labs in Minnesota and Georgia.
Jan. 18, 2009	PCA expanded its recall to include more peanut butter and peanut paste produced on or after July 1, 2008.
Jan. 19, 2009	FDA posted a searchable database so that consumers could identify recalled products.
Jan. 21, 2009	FDA announced that laboratory testing by state officials in Minnesota and Connecticut confirmed that the sources of the outbreak of illnesses caused by *Salmonella Typhimurium* were peanut butter and peanut paste produced by PCA at its Blakely, Georgia, plant.
Jan. 27, 2009	The FDA finished its investigation of the PCA Blakely plant and reported on its inspection with a list of problems.
Jan. 28, 2009	PCA expanded its recall to all peanut products processed in its Blakely facility since Jan. 1, 2007; all production stopped at PCA's Blakely facility.

POST-CRISIS PHASE

Feb. 5, 2009	USDA announced ban on all government contracts for PCA products.
Feb. 8, 2009	PCA announced additional information about recall, and mentioned about the products they directly sold to consumers.
Feb. 13, 2009	PCA filed for Chapter 7 (liquidation of assets) in Western District of Virginia.
Feb. 26, 2009	FDA issued final investigation report.

METHOD

The present study used a case study approach to identify how the events and communication processes pertaining to the food recall and outbreak were portrayed on the company website and in media coverage for PCA. A website search limited to PCA yielded 211 articles. These articles, located on *Lexis-Nexis* database, were downloaded and analyzed. The articles retrieved included national and regional newspapers, news transcripts, press releases, web-based publications, and articles from blogs. Articles ranging in date from January 1st to March 1st were extracted from these sources. Official responses from PCA and government agencies were taken from the articles, as well as company and agency websites. Quotations and information from PCA were taken from these sources and were further analyzed.

The method developed by Littlefield et al. (2012) was used to code the dialectical tensions involved in this case study. These coding criteria helped determine if PCA's responses were immediate or delayed (see Table 2.2). As this case study focused on the dialectical tension of timeliness, a high emphasis was placed upon the dates that PCA communicated with the public.

Table 2.2.   Coding Criteria for Timeliness

Continuum Anchor	Dialectical Tension	Continuum Anchor	Coding Criteria and Coding Examples
Immediate	Timeliness ♦———♦	Delayed	♦ Immediate: Messages are presented immediately to public, upon learning information. (For example: *"This morning, we were informed …"*) ♦ Delayed: Messages are presented to public after a period of time upon learning information. (For example: *"We were informed of this last month …"*)

These dates were then compared to the dates that FDA and USDA issued their findings about the contamination/investigation. Analysis of the data revealed identifiable interactions of dialectical tension of timeliness in PCA during three phases: pre-crisis, crisis, and post-crisis. Articles reporting information unrelated to the Peanut Corporation America's food recall were eliminated from the case study.

RESULTS AND ANALYSIS

Pre-Crisis

In the pre-crisis phase, no direct connection from any agency was made to PCA. However, there is no record that PCA made any preemptive responses during this period about the quality of its products or any potential risks associated with eating their products. According to the CDC, the first reported *Salmonella* infection in this case was reported on September 8, 2008. Then, on November 25, 2008, the CDC began to assess a cluster of salmonella cases that spanned twelve states. The first death was reported on December 21 in a Brainerd, Minnesota, nursing home. After more cases surfaced, on January 8, 2008, the FDA visited the Ohio distributer of PCA. FDA then continued an environmental investigation at the Georgia PCA plant. The investigations by the FDA and CDC determined that the peanut source for King Nut brand peanut butter was the PCA plant located in Blakely, Georgia (FDA, 2009).

Crisis

As the crisis escalated, PCA was reactive in its attempts to be timely. Even when the authorities directly linked the contamination to the company, Parnell and his associates responded after the fact. For example, on January 9, when the Minnesota Department of Health revealed the contamination of the King Nut brand, it was not until the next day that King Nut announced a voluntary recall of its contaminated product (CDC, 2009). On January 9, 2009, in response to the FDA initiating inspections and the sampling of collections with six investigators onsite at PCA's Blakely facility, PCA ceased

Table 2.3. Timing of Multiple Responses

Date	FDA, USDA and Other Organizations Response	PCA's Responses
Jan. 10, 2009	King Nut recalls	
Jan. 13, 2009		PCA recalls
Jan. 17, 2009	FDA notifies PCA that samples are contaminated	
Jan. 18, 2009		PCA expands recall
Jan. 21, 2009	FDA confirm that the sources of the outbreak is PCA	
Jan. 27, 2009	FDA finishes investigation	
Jan. 28, 2009		PCA expands recall
Feb. 8, 2009		PCA mentions about products directly sold to consumers

production and the shipment of peanut paste and powder. On January 13, 2009 (PCA, 2009a), PCA issued its first press release, three days after the investigation began. This press release also introduced Stewart Parnell, who emerged as the main spokesperson throughout the crisis (PCA, 2009a).

Parnell was accessible to the public only through press releases and company statements. His only response in the press releases was: "Out of an abundance of caution, we are voluntarily withdrawing this product and contacting our customers. We are taking these actions with the safety of our consumers as our first priority" (PCA, 2009a). Of particular importance in the statement was the claim that: "none of the peanut butter product recalled is sold directly to consumers through retail stores" (PCA, 2009a).

On January 17, 2009, the FDA announced that it had notified PCA about product samples originating from its Blakely facility that were tested and found positive for *Salmonella* by labs in Minnesota and Georgia (FDA, 2009). The following day, PCA issued its second press release to announce the expansion of the recall (PCA, 2009b). The statement suggested that all peanuts have "[the] potential to be contaminated" (PCA, 2009b). Parnell's comments in this release focused only on the expanded recall and not the FDA's findings (PCA, 2009b). On January 21, the FDA established a link between the deadly outbreak and its source, the peanut butter and peanut paste produced by PCA (FDA, 2009). On January 27, the FDA finished its investigation and identified the set of problems found in the PCA plant that contributed to the contamination. Once again, PCA's response was delayed more than a week. In its press release on January 28, PCA stated that that it was "not aware of any complaints or reports of illness involving the additional peanuts and peanut products" (PCA, 2009c).

Parnell abstained from further comment after the joint statement by the Parnell family and PCA on January 28 (PCA, 2009d). PCA's statement released on January 31 mentioned that employees and attorneys were engaged in understanding the facts and issues of the crisis and concluded by stating that, "any discussion of the facts at this point is premature" (PCA, 2009e). PCA's slowed its release of information to the public as the crisis escalated.

The situation worsened for PCA as media began reporting about the poor sanitary standards at the company. The *New York Times* confirmed: "State inspectors found rust that could flake into food and gaps in warehouse doors big enough for rodents to enter at the Peanut Corporation of America plant" (Harris, 2009). The plant had many hazards related to sanitary conditions, including holes in ceiling, as well as insects and even rodents in their facility (Moss, 2009). PCA never replied to these allegations. On February 2, as news reports of the crisis escalated, President Obama promised a comprehensive review of the FDA, and stated his disappointment on the *Today Show,* saying: "I think that the FDA has not been able to catch some of these things as quickly as I expect them to catch'' (Harris, 2009). News sources later revealed that PCA product recalls extended beyond U.S. borders to both Canada and Europe.

PCA's statement released on February 8 revealed that the company had been selling products directly to consumers (PCA, 2009h). This was contrary to the earlier assurances that PCA had never sold peanut products directly to consumers. The statement revealed: "Consumers should be aware that the list below includes only PCA's own brands that were sold to consumers at retail" (PCA, 2009h). These PCA brands included Casey's, Parnell's Pride, Reggie, and Robinson Crusoe; that were then sold to the public at locations, such as 99 Cent Stuff, 99 Cents Only Stores, Dollar General, and Dollar Tree Stores.

Post-Crisis Phase

PCA lost its credibility with the public due to its failure to respond to the crisis in a timely manner. After the revelations about the direct sales to consumers, the Associated Press reported on February 3 about another plant owned by PCA in Plainview, Texas, that had been uninspected and unlicensed by government health officials for many years (Associated Press, 2009). PCA then responded on February 10, with a press release announcing the temporary suspension of operations of its processing facility in Plainview, Texas (PCA, 2009g). Their delayed press release contained no comments from Parnell or any spokesperson from PCA. On February 12, the Texas Department of State Health Services ordered PCA to cease the manufacture and distribution of all food products from its Plainview, Texas, plant; and to immediately recall all products manufactured there since March 2005 (FDA, 2009). As the events of the crisis further unfolded, PCA filed for bankruptcy on February 13; it was no longer available to communicate with customers about recalled products (PCA, 2009h).

CONCLUSION

PCA failed to handle the crisis effectively; in part, due to its delay in initially notifying distributors about the potential contamination of its products and then later in its response to the findings of the CDC and FDA regarding its link to salmonella and the revelation that consumers were also directly at risk through point of purchase locations. In addition, the failure of PCA to prioritize the immediate release of information had cultural implications due to the status of the consumers of the products.

Initially, PCA was slow in responding to the potential contamination of its products. For example, PCA issued its first press release three days after the investigation began; and it took PCA officials one week to respond when the

FDA firmly established a link between the deadly outbreak and their production facility.

PCA's responses were not only delayed for distributers, but for point of purchase customers as well. In fact, PCA totally ignored point of purchase customers at the beginning of the crisis, insofar as the company initially denied in its January 13 press release ever selling directly to consumers (PCA, 2009a). However the release on February 8 reversed this statement by indicating that PCA did indeed sell to consumers under their own labels, such as Parnell Pride (PCA, 2009f). For nearly a month PCA delayed sharing this vital information with the public and consumers. Thus, for the tension of timeliness, PCA did not prioritize immediacy.

The cultural implications of delaying the timing of the recall were serious because the primary recipients of the bulk products were vulnerable individuals in health care facilities, schools, and other agencies catering to individuals in lower socio-economic groups. The urgency of notifying distributers about the recall should have been recognized by PCA because institutions that used the products did so due to their affordability and adaptability. Moreover, the products could be incorporated into a variety of recipes and meals that were widely distributed to children, patients, and elderly populations. Also of concern is the fact that the press releases issued by PCA were distributed online. This means of dissemination was not appropriate given that those most affected (i.e., vulnerable publics from lower socio-cultural groups) may not have had access to computers to learn about the contamination in the first place.

In addition, the widely held recognition of peanut butter as a source of protein made its sale under PCA labels at dollar stores and low-budget outlets a threat to those who were likely to purchase the products directly. The fact that the victims of the crisis were vulnerable due to their health, economic status, or age made the delay in notification about the potential contamination and ultimate acknowledgment even more offensive to observers.

What makes the tension of timeliness even more critical for companies in risk or crisis situations is the expanded use of social media, such as Facebook and Twitter. Because information can be shared instantly, the expectation of the publics to have immediate access makes any delay in releasing information or responding to the external entities problematic for decision-makers in organizations. The digital landscape and the consumers' ability to share information should not be ignored.

The immediacy of message sharing among publics and between companies and their consumers is another reason risk and crisis messages should be as timely as possibly. On the positive side, blogs and Twitter feeds are already being used by the FDA and CDC, so agencies and organizations can benefit by adapting to these new forms of messaging. On the flip side, because information can be blogged and shared quickly without authentication, agencies and organizations need to monitor and use these mediums to stay ahead of misinformation that may be disseminated by unauthorized spokespeople or those affected by the risk or crisis situation.

Giving a timely message not only shows that an organization is proactive in making decisions about how to manage a risk or crisis situation, but it also shows that consumers are valued. Timeliness can provide an organizational advantage for the crisis decision-maker by staying ahead of other media outlets providing information to concerned publics about the crisis. As was seen in the case of PCA, the delay in responding prompted the media to seek out and uncover more information about PCA, which worsened the crisis. At that point media sources were providing more timely information than PCA.

Where PCA Failed

The tension of timeliness offers immediacy and delay as opposing endpoints on the continuum. While there is no inherent good or bad associated with either end, in this case, PCA's choice to delay its responses resulted in negative ramifications for the company and, ultimately, bankruptcy.

PCA, throughout this crisis, failed to be timely both in its actions and responses. At the time in the crisis when stakeholders needed information, PCA failed to proactively respond. In their studies, Barton (2001) and Coombs (2006) suggested that organizations are better able to handle crises when they have crisis management plans that are regularly updated; have designated crisis management teams; conduct exercises to test the plans at least annually; and pre-draft some crisis messages. Thus, one reason for the reactive press releases coming days or weeks after the initial emergence of the outbreak may have been that PCA was not prepared with a crisis plan. Another reason for the delay may have been related to one of the other tensions in this book; that of *self-interest* versus *other-interest*. In reality, as a best practice, immediate responses enable an organization to generate greater credibility than slow responses (Arpan & Rosko-Ewoldsen, 2005).

Implications for End Users

Knowing when to release information to the publics is often one of the first issues decision-makers confront when facing a risk or crisis situation. Whether the information is released immediately or delayed can affect the perceptions of those who ultimately are impacted by the crisis. If the consumers are making a significant choice or decision that affects their health or safety, they may want to have the information as soon as it is available. On the other hand, if all information is not immediately available, delaying the release of the message may be in the publics' best interests.

Having a crisis management plan and a designated management team is an asset for an organization because if a plan is in place, decision-makers are likely better able to respond quickly than if they have to decide how to manage a crisis while it is occurring. Naming the spokesperson and thinking through potential crises scenarios enables an organization to have drafts of messages in place that can be modified quickly as a crisis situation evolves.

Finally, developing expertise with social media can be an asset for an organization seeking to be ahead of other media outlets when releasing information to those affected by a risk or crisis situation. Updating social media tools on a regular basis will keep the decision-makers apprised of new technological advancements and ways to release information to those seeking information.

REFERENCES

Andrews, J. (2012, April 16). 2009 peanut butter outbreak: Three years on, still no resolution for some. *Food Safety News*. Retrieved from www.foodsafetynews.com.

Arpan, L. M., & Roskos-Ewoldsen, D. R. (2005). Stealing thunder: An analysis of the effects of proactive disclosure of crisis information. *Public Relations Review*, *31*(3), 425–433.

Associated Press. (2009, February 13). *Peanut corp. of America files for bankruptcy*. Retrieved from http://www.chicagotribune.com/topic/la-na-peanut-corp14–2009feb14,0,7701002.story.

Augustine, N. R. (1995). Managing the crisis you tried to prevent. *Harvard Business Review*, *73*(6), 147–158. Harvard Business School Publication Corp. Retrieved from http://ezproxy.library.capella.edu/login?url=http://search.epnet.com/login.aspx?direct=true&db=buh&an=9512052741.

Barton, L. (1991). When managers find themselves on the defensive. *Business Forum*, *16*, 8–13.

Barton, L. (2001). *Crisis in organizations II* (2nd ed.). Cincinnati, OH: College Divisions South-Western.

Baxter, L. A., & Montgomery, B. M. (1996). *Relating: Dialogues and dialects*. New York: Guilford.

Centers for Disease Control and Prevention (CDC). (2009, April 20). *Timeline of infections: Multistate outbreak of salmonella infections associated with peanut butter and peanut butter-containing products—United States, 2008–2009*. Retrieved from http://www.cdc.gov/salmonella/typhimurium/salmonellaOutbreak_timeline.pdf.

Chapman, D., & Newkirk, M. (2009, February 8). *Blakely plant part of firm with humble start*. Retrieved from http://www.ajc.com/services/content/news/stories/2009/02/08/peanutcorp0208.html.

Coombs, W. T. (1999). Information and compassion in crisis responses: A test of their effects. *Journal of Public Relations Research, 11*(2), 125–142. Retrieved from http://www.informaworld.com/10.1207/s1532754xjprr1102_02.

Coombs, W. T. (2006). *Code red in the boardroom: Crisis management as organizational DNA*. Westport, CT: Praeger.

Food and Drug Administration (FDA). (2009, March). Timeline: Salmonella typhimurium investigation. Retrieved from http://www.fda.gov/downloads/Safety/Recalls/MajorProductRecalls/Peanut/FDAâ€™sInvestigation/UCM165790.pdf.

Harris, G. (2009, February 3). Peanut product recall took company approval. *New York Times*, p. 13. Retrieved from the LexisNexis database.

Knerl, L. (2007, December 11). *Peanut butter: The poor man's protein*. Retrieved from http://www.wisebread.com/peanut-butter-the-poor-man-s-protein.

Layton, L. (2009, March 20). Nestle's inspectors saw rat droppings, rejected peanuts. *The Washington Post*. Retrieved from www.washingtonpost.com.

Layton, L., & Miroff, N. (2009, February 19). The rise and fall of a peanut empire. *The Washington Post*. Retrieved from www.washingtonpost.com.

Lee, B. K. (2005). Crisis, culture, community. *Communication Yearbook, 29*: 275–309.

Littlefield, R. S., Farell, L., Beauchamp, K., & Rathnasinghe, S. (2012). Maintaining relationships with the public: Applications of relational dialectics theory in crisis communication. Paper presented at the National Communication Association Convention, Orlando, Florida.

Martinelli, K. & Briggs, W. (1998). Integrating public relations and legal responses during a crisis: The case of Odwalla, Inc. *Public Relations Review, 24*(4), 443–460. Retrieved from http://linkinghub.elsevier.com/retrieve/pii/S0363811199801106.

Moss, M., & Martin, A. (2009, March 6). Food safety problems elude private inspectors. *New York Times*, p. 1. Retrieved from the LexisNexis database.

Peanut butter. (2012). Retrieved from http://www.enotes.com/peanut-butter-reference/peanut-butter-178094.

Peanut Corporation of America (PCA). (2009a, January 13). Peanut Corporation of America announces voluntary nationwide recall of peanut butter. [Press release no longer available online.]

Peanut Corporation of America (PCA). (2009b, January 18). Peanut Corporation of America expands nationwide recall of peanut butter. [Press release no longer available online.]

Peanut Corporation of America (PCA). (2009c, January 28). Peanut Corporation of America expands nationwide recall of peanut products. [Press release no longer available online.]

Peanut Corporation of America (PCA). (2009d, January 28). Statement by the Parnell family and Peanut Corporation of America. [Press release no longer available online.]

Peanut Corporation of America (PCA). (2009e, January 31). Statement by Peanut Corporation of America. [Press release no longer available online.]

Peanut Corporation of America (PCA). (2009f, February 8). Peanut Corporation of America provides additional information about expanded nationwide recall of peanut products. [Press release no longer available online.]

Peanut Corporation of America (PCA). (2009g, February 10). Plainview Peanut Company announces temporary suspension of operations of its processing facility until completion of food safety investigations. [Press release no longer available online.]

Peanut Corporation of America (PCA). (2009h, February 20). Peanut Corporation of America provides further information regarding recalled products. [Press release no longer available online.]

Seeger, M. W. (2006). Best practices in crisis communication: An expert panel process. *Journal of Applied Communication Research, 34*(3), 232–244. doi: 10.1080/00909880600769944.

Severson, K. (2009, January 23). List of tainted peanut butter items points to complexity of food production. *New York Times*, p. 12. Retrieved from the LexisNexis database.

Strong, K. C., Ringer, R. C., & Taylor, S. A. (2001). The rules of stakeholders satisfaction (timeliness, honesty, empathy). *Journal of Business Ethics, 32*(3), 219–230. Springer. Retrieved from http://search.ebscohost.com/login.aspx?direct=true&db=bth&AN=12128520&site=ehost-live.

Chapter Three

The Tension of Openness

An Examination of Menu Foods'
Organizational Disclosure during
the 2007 Pet-Food Recall

Laura C. Farrell

The 2007 Menu Foods pet-food recall offers a crisis example that showcases the dialectical tension organizations face when deciding the *amount of information to reveal* to the public. Menu Foods was the largest producer of wet pet food in North America until 2007 when the company recalled over sixty million containers of pet food contaminated with melamine (Grabowski, 2010). This particular crisis reveals a divide between the organization and consumers' perceptions of responsibility in the crisis. While Menu Foods viewed itself as a victim and denied knowledge of melamine in its products, consumers viewed Menu Foods as entirely responsible, and at fault (Surridge, 2007).

Menu Foods imported wheat gluten adulterated with melamine and cyanuric acid from several Chinese companies (Food and Drug Administration, 2007b). Melamine is an organic base that can be disguised as a protein, but when combined with cyanuric acid may cause renal failure, kidney failure, or death if consumed (Food and Drug Administration, 2007b). The pet-food recall was initiated because melamine was identified in the wheat gluten of pet-food products sold by Menu Foods. Menu Foods perceived itself as a victim because it claimed, "the gluten supplied by ChemNutra was supposed to be safe, and the company had no way of knowing it would contain levels of the chemical Melamine" (Surridge, 2007). Menu Foods spokesperson Sam Bornstein said: "Melamine is something that has no place in any food. It would be like if you bought bananas and tested them for gasoline. Why would you?" (Surridge, 2007).

The magnitude of the pet-food recall was greater than any other food recall to date. Pet owners represented more than 63 percent of U.S. households during the time of the pet-food recall (American Pet Products Association, 2008). The Food and Drug Administration (FDA) received thousands of inquiries (Food and Drug Administration, 2007b), and thousands of pet-food varieties were added to the recall list (Burns, 2007; Food and Drug Administration, 2007c). While Menu Foods most likely meant the best for its consumers, and desired to maintain a favorable relationship, this was not the outcome.

Extensive media coverage during the post-crisis events of the pet-food recall highlighted minimal action and unwillingness to share information on behalf of the pet-food manufacturer, Menu Foods. The public's responses to Menu Foods' nondirective information was outrage and distrust toward the organization, and concern for the health and safety of their pets. In order to understand the complex outcome of the 2007 melamine outbreak and pet-food recall, an examination of the cultural context surrounding the crisis follows.

CULTURAL CONTEXT

The Menu Foods melamine outbreak and pet-food recall was an example of a domestic crisis with international implications. The unique cultural context of this crisis added layers of complexity in the post-crisis phase. While consumers and the public blamed Menu Foods for poor crisis management strategies, Menu Foods blamed the Chinese companies for intentionally contaminating the wheat gluten. This blaming cycle resulted in Menu Foods' misconception of what its consumers and the public needed, in terms of crisis management strategies.

Pet owners have a unique bond with their pets. Pets are considered companion animals, and primary sources of comfort, companionship, and support (Grier, 2006). The term *pet* (derived from the French word "petit") has long been the affectionate term for animals kept for pleasure and companionship (Grier, 2006). To many pet owners, pets are described as part of the family (Bergler, 1988).

Pet owners as a consumer culture also shared another unique quality: social media collaboration. Social media serves as a way for pet owners to connect with other pet owners. The tech-savvy pet owners use social media sites (e.g., Dogbook on Facebook, mycatspace.com, Petster.com) to share stories about their pet animals. Weblogs and social networking sites also provide useful information (e.g., healthcare resources, community events).

Cultural context is a key component in crises situations (Farrell & Littlefield, 2012). To maintain a positive relationship with consumers, organizations must strive to understand how their consumer culture may influence the cultural context of the crisis. In the case of the Menu Foods pet-food recall, the consumer culture was comprised of pet owners who shared a special connection with their pets, and were well connected through social media. Relational dialectics theory provides a way to conceptualize dialogue that emerges from relationships between organizations and their consumers in times of crisis.

CONCEPTUAL FRAMEWORK

A relational approach to organizational communication provides a nuanced perspective that highlights the flexible, ongoing connection organizations hope to build with their consumers. In an organizational setting, crisis communicators have the responsibility to make decisions about how to craft their messages with the purpose of continuing a positive relationship with their stakeholders, and the public. Every time a crisis decision is made, there are a variety of salient dialectical tensions that play a role in the final message strategy. For example, organizational leaders must decide how open to be with their consumers and the public. Competing voices from organizational leaders that comprise this decision may cause the organization's approach to openness shift as the post-crisis unfolds.

While each crisis situation involves the shift of multiple dialectical tensions, this chapter highlights how the amount of information revealed by an organization in crisis can be conceptualized along a continuum of disclosure, ranging from open to closed. The amount of information revealed is defined as, "how much information the organization reveals to the media or public" (Littlefield, Farrell, Beauchamp, & Rathnasinghe, 2012). When an organization chooses to be open, available information is fully disclosed to the public (Littlefield et al., 2012). For example, an organization may explain: "We want consumers to go to our Website, identify the contaminated product, and return or discard the product." Being closed involves available information being kept from the public (Littlefield et al., 2012). An organization may state: "At this point we do not feel comfortable offering any additional information," or "no comment."

Relational dialectics adopts a dialogic approach (Baxter, 2006), which recognizes that individuals gain their meaning from the give-and-take interplay of multiple, competing themes or perspectives (Baxter 2006; Baxter & Montgomery, 1996; Braithwaite & Baxter, 2006). For example, in the discourse of open vs. closed, no one end of the continuum is better or worse than the other; their interplay constitutes what is important, and establishes the relationship. Certain factors, such as consumer culture or intentionality behind the crisis, may play a role in what may be considered more or less appropriate for the particular crisis response.

A dialogic understanding of relationships is particularly useful in crisis situations because communication is context-dependent and requires a multi-dimensional understanding of relationships. Organizational leaders must manage the dialectical tensions surrounding disclosure of information to consumers. While disclosure might create an open and trusting relationship with consumers, too much disclosure might cause negative consumer reactions.

The complex decision about how much to disclose in organizational crisis has been a topic of interest in crisis literature. Full disclosure suggests that a company adopting such a policy may be more apt to be forgiven for its role in a crisis situation (Kaufmann, Kesner, & Hazen, 1994). The "no comment" reaction to a crisis, as in the case of Blockbuster Canada Co. and its public relations firm (GCI Group), demonstrates the negative implications of an organization's decision to withhold information from the public (Menzies, 2005). However, it is difficult to know when an organization has been successful at withholding information. For example, the public knows only of organizations whose crises have been played out in the public arena. What is not seen are those companies that have adopted successful nondisclosure strategies.

International leaders from Institute of Real Estate Management (IREM) explained that there are times when being transparent with the public is critical. As Alexey Belov, CPM, in the context of a report described: "The most important element of reacting to a crime is to resist hiding from it and pretend as if nothing has happened" (International News, 2011, p. 52). Belov added that describing everything to the media accurately and truthfully will encourage other consumers and the public to take all necessary measures to minimize their risk in the crisis directly affecting them. However, as Vuong Cam Sinh, CPM, argued in the context of that same article, disclosure is not always the best option. "Depending on the severity of the crisis event and organizational policy on information disclosure, I will decide which pieces of information, if any, I share with the press" (International News, 2011, p. 53).

RESEARCH QUESTIONS

The dialectical tension surrounding the amount of information revealed in a crisis is complex; literature highlights that while organizational disclosure in a time of crisis has warranted positive results, it may not always be the best option. The relational approach to managing disclosure allows organizational leaders to focus on what is best for the survival of the organization: consumer relationships. In order to elucidate the role of the dialectical tension, *amount of information revealed*, the following research questions were posed:

RQ1: How did Menu Foods navigate the dialectical tension of amount of information revealed when dealing with the 2007 melamine outbreak and pet-food recall?

RQ2: How did the consumer culture of the pet owners affect the ability of Menu Foods to resolve the crisis?

CRISIS TIMELINE

As Menu Foods pet-food recall unfolded, three key phases were noted: 1) outbreak investigations; 2) food recalls; and 3) ability to resume business (Littlefield et al., 2012). These phases represented critical periods where the organization publicly issued statements that affected their relationship with consumers. In phase one, *outbreak investigations,* organizations are typically under pressure to make fast decisions about how to respond publicly to the crisis. In the case of Menu Foods pet-food recall, spokespeople provided minimal information to consumers about the pet-food contamination prior to the recall (Groll, 2007). The organization's successful navigation of the dialectical tension during the outbreak investigation set the stage for the proceeding phases. The *food recall* phase is the second critical period where an organization must decide how to announce the recalls and what additional information to provide. As seen in Table 3.1, Menu Foods issued a series of expanded recalls. In the third phase, *ability to resume business*, an organization must again navigate how much to say to the public regarding its responsibility. Here, Menu Foods emphasized how it was the victim in the crisis, rather than offering information about what had happened or what was being done to mitigate the contamination.

METHOD

The present study identified how the events and communication processes pertaining to the pet-food recalls were portrayed on the company website and in media coverage for Menu Foods. The Menu Foods pet-food recall resulted from a product-driven contamination outbreak caused by melamine. Analysis of articles about the food recall and outbreak revealed identifiable characteristics of dialectical tensions, during three phases specific to outbreak investigations, food recalls, and the ability to resume business.

Data Sources

The data included sixty-five blog articles, twenty newspaper articles, and thirteen media artifacts. The blog articles were gathered from the following blog sites: Thepetconnection.com, Itchmo.com, About.com, Pet Food Tracker, and Howl911. The newspaper articles were identified using ProQuest, Infotrac, and Gale Student Resources in Context Academic Database and were drawn from *Knight Ridder Tribune Business News, McClatchy-Tribune Business News, National Post, St. Louis Post-Dispatch, The National Post, The New York Times, Toronto Star*, and *USA Today*. The media artifacts added depth to the analysis,

Table 3.1. Timeline of 2007 Menu Foods' Recall

Phase	Date	Description
Outbreak Investigations (Phase One)	February 20	Menu Foods received first report of three sick cats.
	March 6	Menu Foods sent pet-food from food trials to Cornell University.
	March 12	Menu Foods learned nine cats involved in the trials died.
Food Recalls (Phase Two)	March 16	Pet-food recall was issue (including over sixty million pet-food cans).
	March 20	FDA confirmed fourteen dead pets.
	March 23	Procter & Gamble was the first to identify melamine in the pet-food.
	March 30	FDA announced melamine as the leading cause of related pet illness/deaths. FDA also announced wheat gluten from China was the source of the melamine in the pet-food products.
	April 5	Menu Foods expanded the original recall.
	April 10	Menu Foods expanded the recall again to include pet food sold in December and January under certain brands
	April 12	Menu Foods expanded the recall to Canadian produced pet food.
	April 16	FDA announced a nationwide investigation tracing eight import entries from the Chinese firm since 2006.
	May 9	China launched a food and drug safety crackdown.
	May 24	U.S. officials requested Chinese officials strive to reach goals related to food safety.
Ability to Resume Business (Phase Three)	June 1	Menu Foods played victim saying the recall was a result of a terrible fraud.
	August 15	Menu Foods lost a major contract with its largest customer, Wal-Mart chain.
	October 11	Menu Foods announced the plan to cut 10–15 percent of its workforce.

(Flavelle, 2007; Groll, 2007; Surridge, 2007)

and included websites and online materials from pet-food industry groups including: Menu Foods, United Pet Groups, American Nutrition, Chenango Valley, U.S. Department of Agriculture, Economic Research Service, marker-research.com, Bizminer, and International Book Import Service World.

The data sources were published between February 2007 and March 2008. The use of public documents is beneficial because the media sources allow researchers to capture language and words of consumers, or the written messages to which consumers were exposed (Creswell, 2009). While a limitation of using public documents is their lack of authenticity or articulation through secondary sources of information, the data were compiled unobtrusively from a variety of sources to provide an unbiased collection of information (Creswell, 2009).

Coding Procedures

The articles and media artifacts were open coded for themes using *a priori* guide of the organizational dialectical tension—amount of information revealed—one of the seven tensions identified by Littlefield et al. (2012) (see Table 3.2).

Using the dialectical continuums anchored by the semantic differentials, open vs. closed, statements and actions of the company were analyzed during the crisis. For example, Menu Foods' statement was considered *open* if the organization publicly disclosed all available information upon receiving facts and notification from agencies. The company's statement was considered *closed* if the organization chose to refrain from disclosing information upon receiving facts and notification from agencies.

Table 3.2. Coding Criteria for Timeliness

Continuum Anchor	*Dialectical Tension*	*Continuum Anchor*	*Coding Criteria and Coding Examples*
Open	Amount of Information Revealed ♦———♦	Closed	♦ Open: Available information is fully disclosed to public. (For example: *"We plan to be fully accessible to the media throughout the investigation."*) ♦ Closed: Available information is kept from the public. (For example: *"We have no comment."*)

RESULTS

Three phases, as reflected by points in time, are used to present the results of the case study analysis of Menu Foods. Phase one (Outbreak Investigations) began when the company realized a suspected link between its pet-food products and a pet-health outbreak. Phase two (Food Recalls) occurred when Menu Foods pet-food products were identified as the cause of the outbreak, and the recall(s) issued. For phase three (Ability to Resume Business), data were analyzed for evidence of the organization's ability to resume business, following the recalls. For each phase, Menu Foods' actions and statements were analyzed using the dialectical-tension coding criteria for amount of information revealed, ranging along the continuum of open to closed.

Outbreak Investigations (Phase One)

In the case of Menu Foods, phase one began late February 2007 when test results confirmed contaminated pet foods were causing pet illnesses and indirect links were made to Menu Foods pet-food products. On February 27, Menu Foods conducted taste tests, feeding its product to forty cats and dogs, and on March 12, nine cats from the testing died (Fergus, 2007). Menu Foods offered no comment during the period the initial link was suggested (Zezima, 2007a).

The public perceived this "no comment" period as an irresponsible move by Menu Foods (Schmit, 2007b; Schmit & Weise, 2007; Zezima, 2007a). As a result, the public questioned Menu Foods' integrity as an organization, and viewed the company as guilty from the beginning (Zezima, 2007a). The media leapt at the chance to report a cover-up, highlighting confused and angry reactions from pet owners. One pet owner, James Byrne, described his cat's death, "She stopped eating and drinking and became so skinny . . . it went really fast. If any family pet passes away, it's hard and traumatic" (Ong, 2007, p. 1).

In lieu of the accusations, Menu Foods backpedaled, claiming that shortly after receipt of the first complaint, the company initiated a battery of technical tests conducted by both internal and external specialists. Organizational spokespeople claimed Menu Foods did not tell the public about these tests because they did not want to cause alarm until they were sure their pet foods were contaminated and causing the illnesses (Menu Foods Income Fund, 2007).

Food Recall (Phase Two)

Menu Food's food recalls were not only severely delayed, once they came out, the information was confusing and scattered for consumers. Menu Foods initiated the first recall on March 16, almost one month after the initial links between Menu Foods' pet-food products and pet illness were identified (Groll, 2007). Approximately two weeks after the initial recalls, media coverage exploded with pet-food recalls and recall updates on hundreds of pet-food brands, both premium and low grade (Food and Drug Administration, 2007a; Groll, 2007; Szabo, 2007). Conflicting information emerged on the types of pet-food brands affected. Initially, only wet pet-food brands were reported as contaminated; later dry pet foods were also reported contaminated. Further, there were contradicting reports about the numbers of pets that had died or were generally affected (Menu Foods Income Fund, 2007; Zezima, 2007a).

The FDA produced an official report on April 6, with fourteen confirmed animal deaths. A massive public outcry and unverified reports of a larger number of pets killed and affected accelerated the crisis (Mann, 2007). FDA received more than 12,000 complaints from concerned pet owners (Food and Drug Administration, 2007b; North Country Gazette, 2007). The number of complaints far exceeded the typical 5,000 complaints over the span of a year (Food and Drug Administration, 2007a).

A lack of trust and consumer confidence in the pet-food industry and FDA surfaced as a result of the organization's poor judgment in disclosure of information pertaining to the crisis. Sakharam Patil, a consultant from S. K. Patil & Associates in Munster, Indiana, said, "Missing such an event shouldn't happen. They [Menu Foods] still have the responsibility of controlling all the ingredients going into their products" (Schmit, 2007a, p. B1). Several consumers were angry at the revelation that a majority of the pet-food brands were produced or co-packed by different pet-food producers (Nestle, 2008). They questioned whether sensitive goods like food and drugs ought to be imported from China at all, and many pet owners transitioned to home cooking for pets (Zezima, 2007a).

The lack of detailed information drew complaints from veterinary experts. Dr. Paul Pion, president and co-founder of the Veterinary Information Network said, "I gotta believe that they [Menu Foods] know more than what they are saying. We need full disclosure if we are going to figure this out. We got to get the company to give out the history of what was needed for the recall" (Sorkin, 2007, p. A1). An FDA spokeswoman said she was unsure whether the company was cooperating. The chief executive officer at Menu Foods and company spokespeople did not return calls seeking comment (Sorkin, 2007).

At this point, company spokespeople could have recognized that consumers perceived their reaction to the crisis negatively. From a relational perspective, a reevaluation of its approach to managing the dialectical tension of open vs. closed may have caused organizational leaders to become more proactive in disseminating any information they had about the melamine outbreak and pet-food recalls. Instead, angry pet owners became self-sufficient in seeking information, and continued to lose trust in Menu Foods.

Several pet owners turned to testing their pet food independently (Pet Food Recall Facts, 2007). Pet owners were skeptical about the test results from the FDA and other sources such as University of California (UC) Davis, accusing UC-Davis of apparent conflict of interest because the university was a beneficiary of a half-million dollar grant from Hill's Pet Company, one of the affected pet-food producers (Pet Food Recall Facts, 2007). One pet owner wrote:

> At this point, with so much lying, so many confidentiality agreements, and a complete lack of regulatory consequences for those responsible for the mass poisoning of our pets, I will never believe any official announcement by any of the players in these disgraceful incidents. (Itchmo, 2007d)

The media and public became overwhelmingly interested in mistakes and cover-ups by the FDA and pet-food industry. The outraged and frustrated pet owners ultimately mobilized into a national network of blogger sites, including The Pet Connection.com, Itchmo.com, PetFoodTracker.com, and ThePetFoodList.com (Weise, 2007a). While the mainstream media focused on breaking news and other significant developments in the story, these bloggers took a different approach of finding what specific details pet owners needed and putting the information all together (Weise, 2007b).

Pet bloggers offered pet owners two simple, easy-to-print, "take-to-the-supermarket" lists of affected pet foods. One list provided all the foods that had been recalled, neatly divided by brand, while another list provided the foods that were safe (Itchmo, 2007a; Keith, 2007; Pet Food Tracker, 2007). The blogs also provided instant news about the recalls as well as news alerts of pet-food recalls. For verification of the recalls, there were up-to-date links to the FDA and pet-food producers' list of recalled foods and information on associated symptoms of melamine poisoning in affected pets (Itchmo, 2007c).

The bloggers were seen by pet owners as a source of unbiased information. Ultimately, by March 30, a few days after Menu Food's initial recalls, some blogs such as Itchmo.com had become a news source with 1.5 million visitors (Weise, 2007b). Other bloggers and owners of sites such as Pet Connection, Howl 911, The Pet-food List, and Pet Food Tracker were also deluged by millions of pet owners who were grieving, venting, or digging for answers (Keith, 2007; Weise, 2007b).

The blogs created online databases where owners listed their pets, symptoms, outcome, and veterinary information (Spadafori, 2007b). They also kept running logs of pet deaths, which to pet owners painted a more accurate picture of the scope of the damage than the official count. For example, by March 30, while the mainstream media, FDA, and Menu Foods still reported only sixteen confirmed deaths from tainted food, Pet Connection's self-reported database released just after the recall was announced was reporting up to 2,407 (1,327 cats; 1,080 dogs) pet-food related deaths (Spadafori, 2007a; Zezima, 2007b). Generally because no official number of pet deaths was released, the blog figures have become the only available source that pet owners believe to be legitimate.

In early May, pet owners mobilized using the blogs for class-action suits. The lawsuits were driven by the question of what Menu Foods knew and when the company knew it. Ben Delong described the transition from grief for his late cat Freddie to anger:

> It turned from being sad about it, to "Oh my God I've poisoned my cat and can't believe this happened," to utter disbelief. They [Menu Foods] knew there was a problem and instead of doing the right thing and recalling pet food, they sat on it for so long. (Fergus, 2007, p. 1)

Itcmo.com, Pet Connection, and Howl911 all provided lawsuit data and links to all the lawsuits filed against Menu Foods (Itchmo, 2007b; Schmit & Weise, 2007). Jay Edelson, a Chicago lawyer, wrote: "Based on what we know now, this is a disaster that could have been stopped" (Fergus, 2007). Menu Foods faced more than 100 lawsuits as a result of the contaminated food. Also, class action plaintiffs filed suit in San Francisco seeking relief under Chinese and state laws targeted at the Chinese company that were identified as suppliers of the tainted ingredients (Itchmo, 2007b).

Ability to Resume Business (Phase Three)

Menu Foods failed to recognize the implications of its decision to be closed initially in the crisis, and then only partially open as the crisis progressed. The organization also failed to realize that consumers and the general public saw Menu Foods as being at fault for the melamine outbreak. On June 1, when Menu Foods claimed itself to be the victim in the melamine outbreak and pet-food recall, pet owners became outraged. The recall of pet-food products was estimated to have cost the company up to $45 million and was a result of a "terrible fraud" perpetrated against the company (Surridge, 2007, p. FP5). A spokesperson from Menu Foods alleged the gluten supplied by ChemNutra was supposed to be safe, and Menu Foods had no way of knowing it would contain melamine. A spokesperson from ChemNutra responded to this accusation, saying:

> There has been a terrible fraud committed by the Chinese company whose CEO has been arrested, and of course Menu foods has an obligation to try to recover from its part of this situation by any legal means available. We remain hopeful we can resolve any disagreement with Menu Foods without going to court. (Surridge, 2007, p. FP5)

Menu Foods CEO Paul Henderson said that while the recall could weigh on the company's performance in the next quarter, "it will recover, and the intent will be that we will continue to be around" (Surridge, 2007, p. FP5).

While Henderson was focusing on the financial status of the company, he did not consider the damage that had been done to the relationship between the organization and its consumers. Menu Foods had deeply betrayed its consumers. The closed approach adopted by Menu Foods throughout the majority of the outbreak investigations and recalls resulted in consumer distrust, which escalated into anger and rage.

In mid-August, Menu Foods received a verbal notice that it would lose another major contract from its largest customer, the Wal-mart chain. Menu Foods issued a public statement explaining its disappointment in the reaction of Wal-mart to the pet-food recall. Henderson opined, "The intentional tainting of product inputs from a third-party supplier in China was a fraudulent act that victimized many pet food manufacturers, customers, and consumers" (Menu Foods Looses, 2007).

The company continued to struggle into the fall of 2007 as it had lost 37 percent of its sales since the recall began due to the cancellation of orders by retailers and branded pet-food makers (Flavelle, 2007). On October 11, Menu Foods announced it planned to reduce its workforce by 10 to 15 percent and reduce the pay of company executives. Henderson agreed to a 22 percent reduction, and other executives took a 17 percent reduction (Flavelle, 2007).

CONCLUSION

A relational approach to crisis communication offers a nuanced method of understanding consumer reactions in crisis situations. Ultimately, the relational approach illuminates reasons for the success or failure of an organization's post-crisis management. This study explored Menu Foods' approach to the dialectical tension of openness in the case of the 2007 melamine outbreak and pet-food recall. The case study approach revealed attempts made by the organization to manage the crisis and address the public's concerns. However, Menu Foods did not assess the unique consumer culture of pet owners and their pets. Pet owners clearly demonstrated the inadequacy of Menu Foods' approach to disclosure of information pertaining to the crisis through their escalating outrage toward the company.

A common question voiced by consumers was "why didn't you tell us?" In order to maintain a favorable relationship with its consumers, Menu Foods should have been more open with its stakeholders, even if all the facts and details were not yet confirmed. Alternatively, the company could have been strategically ambiguous, while still appearing to be open. A greater amount of disclosure would have shown that Menu Foods was in fact taking precautions, reducing risk, and rectifying the situation. Instead, the company chose to withhold information from angry pet owners until after the initial melamine outbreak had been confirmed.

While Menu Foods was withholding information and waiting until it was absolutely sure of the outbreak source, pet owners turned to each other using online resources. Concerned pet owners wanted to know what they should, or should not, feed their pet animals, and symptoms to watch for in their pets. The blogs and online communities served as trustworthy and credible sources of information (Peters, Covello, & McCallum, 1997). Official sources became less credible as they failed to share the necessary information with pet owners.

Results of this study are useful particularly to organizations seeking to identify their primary consumers. If Menu Foods had considered its primary consumers' unique culture, the company might have realized pet owners would be concerned and angry when their pets became ill or died. If Menu Foods had treated its relationship with consumers properly, it would have been more receptive to their needs. The organization's most common justification for its unwillingness to disclose information at the onset of the crisis was linked to organizational leaders' desire to be absolutely certain before releasing information (Fergus, 2007). What did not occur to organizational leaders was the concern of pet owners for answers about the contamination, and updates about Menu Foods' investigations and efforts. From a practical standpoint, pet owners also needed confirmation about what they could or could not feed their pet animals. Menu Foods' inability to recognize both the emotional and practical needs of pet owners set the stage for the deconstruction of the organization-consumer relationship.

Strategies for End Users

Organizations continue to exist because of communicative relationships maintained between the organization, stakeholders, and their publics. The ten best practices of risk and crisis communication represent recommended ways for organizations to foster relationships with their stakeholders and the public (Seeger, 2006). If the goal of an organization is driven by its desire to maintain a positive relationship with stakeholders and the public, the primary focus of an organization should be on managing the dialectical tensions that emerge within crisis situations. The best practices create a foundation from which to confront and manage a crisis, and "take the form of a general set of standards, guidelines, norms, reference points or benchmarks that inform practice and are designed to improve performance" (Seeger, 2006, p. 233).

Beauchamp and Littlefield (2012) explained that emphasis on certain best practices shifts as a crisis unfolds, creating a series of interaction combinations where key best practices emerge to the forefront during the crisis. A relational approach to crisis situations aligns with tenets of the best practices, which are typically focused on retaining a positive connection with the public or stakeholders. However by adopting relational dialectics, one can begin to understand, explore, and analyze how the shift in dialogue between the organization and its consumers constitutes their ongoing relationship after the post-crisis.

Relational dialectics emphasizes that individuals gain meaning from the give-and-take interplay of multiple perspectives (Baxter 2006; Baxter & Montgomery, 1996; Braithwaite & Baxter, 2006). Within the discourse of open vs. closed, no one end of the continuum is better or worse than the other. Rather the interplay is what is important, and constitutes the relationship. During the post-crisis, an organization may shift back-and-forth between being more open in their response to the public to more closed. The organization's leaders are faced with the challenge of managing the dialectical tensions surrounding the ideal amount of disclosure of information to consumers. A clear understanding of the role of culture will provide organizational leaders with the edge in making the right decision to disclose.

Consumer culture is one key factor that organizational leaders should consider when determining what may or may not be considered appropriate for the particular crisis response. Menu Foods may have benefited from being more open with its pet-owner consumers. A more open approach may have yielded a drastically different outcome for the company. Pet owners were compelled to turn to each other through blog sites because they did not trust Menu Foods' recommendations. The original mistrust stemmed from the company's hesitation to provide information at the onset of the crisis. Once Menu Foods did provide more information regarding the specifics of recall products and sources of the contamination, pet owners had already lost trust in the company. Even though Menu Foods shifted its emphasis from more closed to more open, evidence suggests that the relationship between the organization and its consumers was already damaged.

While openness is linked to creating positive relational outcomes including, feelings of trust, providing a sufficient level of knowledge, or confidence in accuracy of information, there are instances when disclosure may not be best for an organization's relationship with its consumers. Consumers in crisis may be experiencing heightened emotions, and may be overly sensitive to any information about the crisis. Thus, while it is important to be open with consumers about the crisis, equally important is the need to provide only information that is accurate, and will not induce panic. Additionally, too much information about a crisis may be overwhelming to certain consumer cultures, and may increase the chances of conflicting or confusing information. Consumer culture should ultimately drive an organization's strategy in deciding how to manage the dialectical tension of amount of information revealed.

Public relations and marketing strategies often pay particular attention to consumer culture and target audiences. Particular demographic and psychographic characteristics of consumers guide how an organization or company crafts campaigns and advertisements to market its products. Interestingly, while organizations tend to be particularly sensitive to consumer culture when revenue is the goal, that sensitivity seems to be diminished in the heat of a crisis. Organizational leaders would benefit from becoming even more sensitive to their consumer culture during times of crisis. Putting the organization-consumer relationship at the forefront of crisis communication strategies will help guide organizational leaders in making the right decision about how much information their consumers need.

The end goal of every crisis situation is to return to a state of *new normal* where the organization and consumers have a strengthened relationship and commitment toward each other. This can only be accomplished through the successful navigation of dialectical tensions. An organization's ability to make appropriate choices regarding the amount of information revealed in a crisis directly impacts the organization's relationship with its consumers. The nature and quality of that relationship is what determines the fate of the organization after post-crisis.

REFERENCES

American Pet Products Association. (2008). *APPMA national pet-owners survey.* Greenwich, CT: American Pet Product Association.

Baxter, L. A. (2006). Relational dialectics theory: Multivocal dialogues of family communication. In D. O. Braithwaite & L. A. Baxter (Eds.), *Engaging theories in family communication: Multiple perspectives* (pp. 130–145). Thousand Oaks, CA: Sage.

Baxter, L. A., & Montgomery, B. M. (1996). *Relating: Dialogues and dialectics.* New York: Guilford.

Beauchamp, K. A., & Littlefield, R. S. (2012). The Maple Leaf Foods recall: Best practice interaction during a food-related crisis. *International Journal of Business Continuity and Risk Management, 3*(1), 1–18. doi: 10.1504/IJBCRM.2012.045524.

Bergler, R. (1988). *Man and dog: The psychology of a relationship.* Oxford, UK: Blackwell Scientific.

Braithwaite, D. O., & Baxter, L. A. (2006). "You're my parent, but you're not": Dialectical tensions in stepchildren's perceptions about communication with the nonresidential parent. *Journal of Applied Communication Research, 24,* 30–48. doi: 10.1080/00909880500420200.

Burns, K. (2007). Recall shines spotlight on pet-foods. *Journal of American Veterinary Medical Association, 230,* 1285–1288.

Creswell, J. W. (2009). Research design: Qualitative, quantitative, and mixed method approaches (3rd ed.). Thousand Oaks, CA: Sage.

Farrell, L. C., & Littlefield, R. S. (2012). Identifying communication strategies in cases of domestic terrorism: Applying cultural context to the Fort Hood Shooting. *The Journal of Homeland Security and Emergency Management, 9*(1), doi: 10.1515/1547-7355.

Fergus, M. A. (2007, April 1). Class-action lawsuit charges pet-food company with fraud. *McClatchy-Tribune News Service,* p. 1. Retrieved from ProQuest Newsstand (Document ID: 456502844).

Flavelle, D. (2007, October 11). Menu raises recall costs, to slash jobs. *Toronto Star,* p. B3. Retrieved from ProQuest Newsstand (Document ID: 439321548).

Food and Drug Administration. (2007a, April 16). *Pet-food recall: FDA's ongoing investigation: US Department of Health and Human Services.* Retrieved from www.fda.gov/ForConsumers/ConsumerUpdates/ucm048192.htm.

Food and Drug Administration. (2007b, June 25). *Melamine pet-food—2007 recall list: US Department of Health and Human Services.* Retrieved from www.accessdata.fda.gov/scripts/petfoodrecall/.

Food and Drug Administration. (2007c, October 7). *Melamine pet-food recall frequently asked questions: US Department of Health and Human Services.* Retrieved from www.fda.gov/AnimalVeterinary/SafetyHealth/RecallsWithdrawals/ucm1292.htm.

Grabowski, G. (2010). The year of the recall response: Case studies in food protection. *Levick Strategic Communications, Global High Stakes Communication.* Retrieved from www.levick.com/index.php?id=1&action=showitem&type=articles&id=170.

Grier, K. (2006). *Pets in America: A history.* New York: Harvest Books, Harcourt.

Groll, M. (2007, April 16). How pet-food recall unfolded. *USA Today.* Retrieved from www.us atoday.com/money/industries/2007–04–05–petfood-timeline-usat_N.htm.

International News: IREM International members share their crisis communication strategies. (2011). *Journal of Property Management, 52–53.* Retreived from www.irem.org/jpm.

Itchmo. (2007a, March 17). Pet-food recall [Blog]. Retrieved from http://www.itchmo.com/pet-food-recall-150.

Itchmo. (2007b, March 19). Menu Foods class action being organized [Blog]. Retrieved from http://itchmo.wordpress.com/2007/03/19/menu-foods-class-action-being-organized/.

Itchmo. (2007c, March 21). Petition to require pet-food companies to be held accountable for damages [Blog]. Retrieved from http://www.itchmo.com/petition-to-require-pet-food-companies-to-be-held-financially-liable-for-pet-deaths-190/comment-page-4/.

Itchmo. (2007d, June 27). ASPCA believes fear of acetaminophen in pet-food to be unfounded [Blog]. Retrieved from http://www.itchmo.com/aspca-believes-fear-of-acetaminophen-in-pet-food-to-be-unfounded-1401.

Kaufmann, J. B., Kesner, I. F., & Hazen, T. L. (1994). The myth of full disclosure: A look at organizational communications during crises. *Business Horizons, 37*(4), 29–39.

Keith, C. (2007, March 31). Pet-food recall: And now, Purina joins the recall [Blog]. Retrieved from http://www.petconnection.com/blog/2007/03/31/pet-food-recall-and-now-purina-joins-the-recall/.

Littlefield, R. S., Farrell, L. C., Beauchamp, K. A., & Rathnasinghe, S. (2012). Maintaining relationships with the public: Applications of relational dialectics theory in crisis situations. Paper presentation at the meeting of the 2012 National Communication Association, Orlando, Florida.

Mann, J. (2007, May 4). Contaminant is confirmed in FDA tests. *Knight Ridder Tribune Business News.* Retrieved from ProQuest Newsstand (Document ID: 1265495221).

Menu Foods Income Fund. (2007, March 16). Menu Foods income fund announces precautionary dog and cat food recall [Press Release]. Retrieved from http://www.menufoods.com/RECALL/Press_Recall_03162007.htm.

Menu Foods loses another contract with top customer. (2007, August 15). *Toronto Star,* p. B6. Retrieved from ProQuest Newsstand (Document ID: 03190781).

Menzies, D. (2005). Silence ain't golden. *Marketing Magazine, 110*(26), 15–18.

Nestle, M. (2008). *Pet-food politics: The Chihuahua in the coalmine.* London: University of California Press.

North Country Gazette. (2007, April 7). Pet-food recall update, FDA says no evidence human food tainted. Retrieved from http://www.northcountrygazette.org/articles/2007/040707RecallUpdate.html.

Ong, B. (2007, March 1). Pet food recall has owners anxious. *McClatchy-Tribune Business News,* p. 1. Retrieved from ProQuest Newsstand (Document ID: 464012452).

Peters, R. G., Covello, V. T., & McCallum, D. B. (1997). The determinants of trust and credibility in environmental risk communication: An empirical study. *Risk Analysis, 17*(1), 43–54.

PetFoodRecallFacts.com (2007, October 11). Independent lab test results. Retrieved from, http://www.petfoodrecallfacts.com/lab.html.

PetFoodTracker.com (2007, March 28). Recalled pet-food tracker [Blog]. Retrieved from, http://localhostr.com/files/3c87768e1d1c3ac43614.pdf.

Schmit, J. (2007a, April 12). "Mistake" caused delay in latest pet-food recall: Possible tainted wheat gluten shipped to plant in Canada. *USA Today,* p. B1. Retrieved from ProQuest Newsstand (Document ID: 409011014).

Schmit, J. (2007b, May 4). More pet-food recalled after discovery: Cross contamination at manufacturers blamed. *USA Today.* Retrieved from ProQuest Newsstand (Document ID: 1265396241).

Schmit, J., & Weise, E. (2007). Pet firms suspend China business: Import scrutiny up after recalls. *USA Today.* Retrieved from ProQuest Newsstand (Document ID: 1274676141).

Seeger, M. W. (2006). Best practices in crisis communication: An expert panel process. *Journal of Applied Communication Research, 34*(3), 232–244.

Sorkin, M. D. (2007, March 20). Wheat gluten suspected in pet food recall veterinarians complained about dearth of information. *St. Louis Post-Dispatch,* p. A1. Retrieved from ProQuest Newsstand (Document ID: 403080780).

Spadafori, G. (2007a, March 22). Pet-food recall: Thursday-morning numbers [Blog]. Retrieved from http://www.petconnection.com/blog/2007/03/22/pet-food-recall-the-latest-numbers/.

Spadafori, G. (2007b, April 26). Pet-food recall: Timing and triggers [Blog]. Retrieved from http://www.petconnection.com/blog/2007/04/26/pet-food-recall-timing-and-triggers/.

Surridge, G. (2007, June 01). Menu foods calls recall "terrible fraud"; Loss may hit $45–Million. *National Post,* p. FP5. Retrieved from ProQuest Newsstand (Document ID: 330553159).

Szabo, L. (2007, March 19). Pet-food recall affects 90 brands; 10 animals dead; cause still sought. *USA Today.* Retrieved from ProQuest Newsstand (Document ID: 1237737111).

Weise, E. (2007a, May 6). Pet-owning bloggers mobilize on food front. *USA Today.* Retrieved from http://www.usatoday.com/tech/webguide/internetlife/2007–06–04–pet-blog-centerpiece_N.htm.

Weise, E. (2007b, June 5). Pet-food scandal ignites blogosphere. *USA Today.* Retrieved from http://ic.galegroup.com.proxy.library.ndsu.edu/ic/suic/NewsDetailsPage/NewsDetailsWindow?

Zezima, K. (2007a, March 22). Pets' owners angered by delays in response. *New York Times.* Retrieved from http://www.nytimes.com/2007/03/22/us/22petfood.html?ref=petfoodrecall.

Zezima, K. (2007b, March 24). Rat poison found in pet-food linked to 14 deaths. *New York Times.* Retrieved from http://query.nytimes.com/gst/fullpage.html?res=9B06E2D9163FF936A35757C0A9619C8B63&ref=petfoodrecall.

Chapter Four

The Tension of Certainty

The Mistakes of the E. coli *Outbreak in Europe*

Nigel D. Haarstad and Robert S. Littlefield

In May 2011, Germany quickly found itself at the epicenter of the largest outbreak of *E. coli* in modern history. The new, highly toxic strain of *E. coli* spread rapidly and led to an unprecedented number of illnesses and deaths among residents of northern Germany, as well as citizens of ten other countries who had recently visited the country. From the first reported death on May 24, until German health officials declared an end to the crisis on July 26, 52 people had died while as many as 4,300 had fallen ill (Germany: E. coli outbreak is over, 2011, July 27).

The responsibility for protecting public health in Germany is shared between state-level ministries and the federal level Robert Koch Institute (Crossland, 2011). This shared responsibility, as well as a rapidly evolving investigation into the cause of the outbreak, led to a number of confusing and sometimes contradicting statements aimed at the public. For example, authorities on more than one occasion expressed confidently that they had determined the source of the outbreak, only to retract the statements when their claims were proven false. As a result of the uncertainty this communication caused, consumer demand for produce plummeted. Tempers flared as produce sales dropped, and the crisis was exacerbated as farmers expressed outrage over the response: "We farmers are furious, very angry, and indignant because we see no explanation for us to be treated this way on the basis of unfounded information" (Brown, 2011). Ultimately, the economic impacts that resulted from these misstatements were blamed on German health authorities, and prompted growers to petition the European Union for a compensation package worth $323.9 million (Cooper, 2011).

Calls for reform were immediate both from within Germany and from other European Union member states. Many German commentators pointed to the fact that there is no central authority in charge of crisis management for public health emergencies, leading to fragmented communication. Others, such as EU health chief John Dalli, accused health officials of confusing the public by issuing premature and inaccurate statements (Dempsey, 2011). This chapter explores how German health officials communicated uncertainty to the public during the *E. coli* crisis.

CULTURAL CONTEXT

The outbreak of *E. coli* in Germany started as a national level crisis, but quickly spread to involve other nations, including Spain and Russia, among others. Although German health officials' communication was aimed squarely at their own citizens, the economic and political repercussions of that communication quickly drew other countries into the dialogue. Further complicating the response, the scope of the crisis included countries with different worldviews and cultural characteristics. Long-standing tensions between Germany and poorer European Union countries, such as Spain, quickly took center stage in the public communication about the outbreak. As this dialogue progressed, German health officials' communication continued to be aimed at and influenced by cultural norms within their own country.

This crisis occurred during a period of economic and political tension in the European Union. By this time, economic crises had forced the governments of Spain, Ireland, Portugal, and Greece to accept financial support from other EU members. The bailouts had a noticeable impact on European politics. The demands of financial institutions and the governments providing capital to the rescue fund became entangled in democratic institutions across the continent (Hallinan, 2011). This quickly led to widespread political resentment from leaders and citizens in Spain, who did not agree with the economic conditions that were imposed on their country by banks and the EU as part of the bailout (Hallinan, 2011). Meanwhile, many in Germany were unhappy about putting taxpayers' money at risk to save Euro-zone countries that had run into trouble because of unsustainable borrowing (Walker & Karnitschnig, 2010). This situation created a tense, often adversarial environment between Germany and Spain; an animosity that would later contribute to the communication practices used during the German *E. coli* outbreak.

THEORETICAL UNDERPINNINGS

This case study focuses on the dialectical tension of *certainty* to understand how it influenced the perception of risk during the German *E. coli* outbreak. In this chapter, certainty is discussed as both a component of Relational Dialectics Theory (RDT), as well as one of the ten best practices for risk communication developed by the National Center for Food Protection and

Defense. RDT offers a conceptual framework to explore various dialectical tensions emerging from crisis situations. One such tension involves a level of certainty that is communicated during a crisis (Littlefield, Farrell, Beauchamp, & Rathnasinghe, 2012). Essentially, this component of the theory states that communicators must choose the amount of certainty/uncertainty to include in their message in order to achieve their goals. For example, an organization may express absolute certainty by saying "We have identified 100 percent of the retail product links to the contamination." On the other end of the spectrum, an organization may express uncertainty with statements, such as: "We may never know the cause of the contamination."

As a component of RDT, the dialectical tension of certainty has often been studied in terms of interpersonal and family communication. However, the component of certainty is equally capable of providing insight into the tensions that are present in relationships between organizations and stakeholders during a crisis (Littlefield et al., 2012). A number of case studies also have examined the use of uncertainty in risk and crisis communication (Sellnow, Ulmer, Seeger, & Littlefield, 2009). This chapter builds on previous studies, by revealing the role of uncertainty and cultural context in the crisis communication efforts of German health officials.

The ten best practices of crisis communication provide a framework by which organizations can improve their communication with the public (Seeger, 2006). One of these practices, *accepting ambiguity and uncertainty*, is particularly relevant to the German *E. coli* outbreak. Ambiguity is achieved by communicating in such a way that the message can support multiple interpretations of a situation at the same time (Weick, 1995). In this case study and other crisis situations, using strategic ambiguity and accepting uncertainty allows officials to maintain credibility and legitimacy during the crisis when not all of the information is known (Sellnow & Ulmer, 2004). Through understanding how German health officials dealt with the *E. coli* outbreak, the utility of accepting uncertainty in risk and crisis communication will become clear.

RESEARCH QUESTIONS

Understanding the role of uncertainty during the 2011 *E. coli* outbreak in Germany provides a useful example of this concept in practice. In order to focus our study of the response to this outbreak, this chapter will concentrate on the following two research questions:

RQ1: How did German health officials navigate the dialectical tension of certainty when dealing with the *E. coli* crisis?

RQ2: How did the cultural context affect the ability of German health officials to resolve the crisis?

METHOD

This analysis used the case study method to develop descriptions of how the events and communication processes pertaining to the *E. coli* outbreak were portrayed in the media. Analysis of articles about the outbreak revealed identifiable characteristics of the dialectical tension of certainty. Through a case study approach, this study identified interactions between the public, messages from German health officials, and the cultural context during the pre-crisis, crisis, and post-crisis stages of the outbreak. Results were analyzed to determine and assess the degree of certainty communicated in statements by German health officials at the state and national level.

Database

A search of the *Lexis-Nexis* database for the terms "Germany *E. coli*" and "German health official" yielded 364 articles. After eliminating duplicates

Table 4.1. Crisis Timeline for 2011 German and European *E. Coli* Outbreak

Date	Event
	Pre-crisis
mid May	*E. coli* outbreak begins.
May 24	One dead, 400 sickened. Source of contamination unknown.
	Crisis
May 26	German health officials implicated cucumbers from Spain as a potential source. Supermarkets begin to pull Spanish cucumbers. German officials advised against eating raw cucumbers, lettuce, and tomatoes.
May 30	Russia suspended imports of cucumbers, lettuce, and tomatoes from the European Union.
May 31	Spanish cucumbers cleared as a source of the outbreak.
June 1	Spain estimated €200 million lost in produce exports. Sixteen now dead, 1,200 sickened.
June 3	Facing complaints from other EU nations about the German response to the outbreak, Chancellor Angela Merkel defended health officials' warning regarding cucumbers.
June 5	Germans told to avoid bean sprouts. German farm identified as likely source of contamination.
June 6	German health officials released test results showing no E. coli at German farm.
	Post-crisis
June 10	Sprouts from German farm determined to be the source of the outbreak. Warning lifted against cucumbers, lettuce, and tomatoes.
June 11	Thirty dead, 3,000 sickened.
July 26	Robert Koch Institute declared outbreak over. Fifty-two deaths, 4,321 sickened.

and unrelated articles, a total of 256 were downloaded and analyzed. These included: television transcripts; Associated Press, international, national, and regional newspaper articles; and blogs. Articles ranging in date from May 23, 2011 to August 5, 2011, were extracted from English-language sources. Quotations and information related to the German *E. coli* outbreak were taken from sources that were either first to report the details or presented a more comprehensive account of the event.

Coding

The articles collected from the search were analyzed for statements attributed to German health officials associated with state-level and federal agencies. Statements regarding the outbreak were coded as "certain" if the officials expressed a high level of confidence in the information they communicated to the public. Messages were coded as "uncertain" if they avoided specifics or if they emphasized the uncertainty of the information revealed to the public. For example, a statement emphasizing certainty may say, "we are confident that the outbreak is over." An uncertain statement would include statements such as, "we do not yet have all the facts" (see Table 4.2).

Table 4.2.   Coding Criteria for Certainty of Information Reported

Continuum Anchor	Dialectical Tension	Continuum Anchor	Coding Criteria and Coding Examples
Certain	Confidence of Information Revealed ♦——————♦	Uncertain	♦ Certain: Organization expresses certainty of the information revealed to the public. (For example: *"Lab results have identified a link to our product . . ."*) ♦ Uncertain: Organization expresses uncertainty of the information revealed to the public. (For example: *""We may never know the cause . . ."*)

RESULTS AND ANALYSIS

Three phases are used to present the results of the case study analysis of the German *E. coli* outbreak. These phases include the pre-cises, crisis, and post-crisis stages. The pre-crisis stage began when the outbreak was identified. In this study, the crisis stage began when the first connection between the problem and the source was identified. Post-crisis refers to the point when the source of the outbreak was confirmed. For each phase, the actions and the messages of German health officials at the state and national levels were analyzed, focusing on the amount of certainty and/or uncertainty communicated in each message.

Pre-Crisis

The pre-crisis stage of the German *E. coli* crisis began in mid-May 2011, when hospitals in northern Germany began to report a surge in infections. By way of context, around 800 to 1,200 cases of *E. coli* sickness are recorded in Germany each year, predominantly affecting children. In this case, during one week in May 2011, over 200 confirmed cases had been identified (Wendel & Wegener, 2011). Health officials noted at the time, that the outbreak was causing unusually severe symptoms and mostly affected adults (Trauner, Frey, & Kusidlo, 2011). German health officials at the state and national level indicated that they did not yet know the source of the contamination, but were actively investigating. Although raw poultry, meat, and contaminated water are often the source of *E. coli* outbreaks, officials suspected that the source came from raw uncooked salad vegetables ("Outbreak of E. coli," 2011).

During the pre-crisis stage, statements released by German health officials were marked by uncertainty: "This outbreak has got no historical precedent," reported one health official from the state of Schleswig-Holstein (Wendel & Wegener, 2011). The Robert Koch Institute, Germany's national center for disease control and prevention, also emphasized that the source of the bacteria was uncertain, and that the outbreak was different from previous *E. coli* outbreaks, explaining that it was not affecting the demographics usually associated with the bacteria ("Outbreak of E. coli," 2011). This "raised questions" about whether the source was a product marketed toward women ("Germany sees a sharp upswing," 2011).

Government health officials continued to emphasize uncertainty throughout the pre-crisis stage. Even as the investigation closed in on raw vegetables as a potential source, health officials declared that, "the source hasn't been discovered"; and the Robert Koch Institute stressed that, "vegetables have not been definitively identified" as the source ("Germany sees a sharp upswing," 2011). These statements clearly demonstrated the uncertainty inherent in the communication of health officials during the pre-crisis phase.

During the pre-crisis stage, German health officials became aware of a significant increase in cases of *E. coli*-related illness. While various state ministries of health and the Robert Koch Institute initiated their investigations, all communication directed toward the public used statements of uncertainty.

At this point in time, statements made by officials focused on what made the outbreak unusual from other cases, as well as the potential for contamination from a wide variety of foods.

Crisis

The crisis stage began when the first connection between the problem and the source was publicly identified. On May 26, German health officials stated that they had identified organic cucumbers from Spain as "one of the confirmed sources responsible" for the outbreak ("Cucumbers blamed," 2011). German supermarkets immediately began to pull Spanish cucumbers off the shelves following the announcement. Hamburg's health minister, Cornelia Prufer-Storcks, said: "it can't be ruled out that other products will come into question as the source of infection" (Pidd Berlin, 2011).

From May 26 through May 31, health officials warned the public that cucumbers were the source of the deadly strain of bacteria. Very little uncertainty was reported in the media regarding these statements. At the same time, health officials were advising consumers to avoid not only cucumbers, but tomatoes and lettuce as well. This led to some confusion about the true cause of the outbreak and also raised concerns about the effectiveness of the response, in general (Crossland, 2011). Throughout this period of time, messages about the source of the outbreak, as well as messages about avoiding other vegetables, were communicated with a high level of certainty.

In an abrupt reversal, German health officials declared on May 31 that Spanish cucumbers were not the source of the particular strain of *E. coli* impacting Germans. Unlike the previous five days, communication from health agencies was now marked by a high level of uncertainty. Reuters quoted an unnamed German official who disclosed that, "The source of the virulent strain of bacteria is unknown" (Kelsey, 2011). Similarly, Hans-Joachim Breetz warned, "it can take days or weeks to find a source of infection" (Hackenbroch, Shafy, & Thadeusz, 2011). Reinhard Burger, head of the Robert Koch Institute, furthered this line of uncertainy, stating that the precise source of the disease outbreak may never be found. He told a European Parliament committee that, "There is still no indication of a definable source" ("Russia bans EU vegetables," 2011). Clearly, officials from various agencies were steering clear of making any definitive assertions about the outbreak, incorporating a high level of uncertainty in their communication.

As new developments arose in the investigation, communication from the various health agencies began to diverge; some institutions created messages with certainty, while others communicated with near-absolute uncertainty. For example, the Hamburg Ministry of Health reported on June 3 that the outbreak was "likely" caused by a source in Germany, demonstrating some certainty ("Killer E. coli," 2011). At the same time, however, the Robert Koch Institute reported that the source had not yet been narrowed down, emphasizing uncertainty (Bronst, 2011). The perception of certainty was also complicated by the continued advisory against eating lettuce, tomatoes, and cucumbers. Officials in northern provinces continued to recommend that the public avoid these foods, while ignoring other types of food that were more commonly attributed to E. coli, such as raw milk and meat (Gale, 2011). Some sources pointed to a contradiction between the certainty of statements regarding these vegetables and the uncertainty communicated in the investigation, as a whole. For example, farmers and grocers questioned the validity of the advisories against eating these three vegetables, pointing out that no link had been established between these foods and the outbreak. The divergent level of certainty among the different agencies, as well as the different level of certainty used to communicate about food advisories versus the investigations, led to confusion among the public.

Shortly thereafter, German health officials at the state level declared with certainty that bean sprouts from a German farm was the cause of the outbreak: "A connection has been found involving all the main outbreaks," said Gert Lindermann, Agriculture Minister for the state of Lower Saxony ("Bean sprouts 'Connection,'" 2011). Lindermann continued, advising Germans to "not eat any bean sprouts right now" ("Bean sprouts 'Connection,'" 2011). Other officials echoed this response: "bean sprouts have been identified as the products that likely caused the outbreak. Many restaurants that suffered from any E. coli outbreak had the sprouts delivered. All indications speak to them being [the cause]" (Grieshaber & Skaro, 2011).

The following day, the same agency reported that test results from the identified farm showed no signs of E. coli ("Germany says," 2011). Although these test results did not mean that the farm was the source, the significance (or lack of significance) of the results was not communicated. Therefore, it appeared as if German health officials were communicating with certainty once again. At this point, the European Union health minister scolded German health officials, ordering them to stop giving inaccurate statements to the public (Cheng & Baetz, 2011).

For the remainder of the investigation into the German farm and the source of the E. coli, communication was marked by clear uncertainty. For example, Federal Health Minister Daniel Bahr said in a television broadcast, "we have clear indication that a farm in the district of Uelzen is a likely source of the contamination, but we must first wait for the results of the laboratory tests"

("Germany probes sprouts," 2011). The Robert Koch Institute, in a statement about the same test results, stated that, "a conclusion of the investigations and a clarification of the contamination's origin is not expected in the short term" (Dempsey, 2011). Once again, health officials had switched to emphasizing uncertainty in their public communication.

Post-Crisis Stage

Relevant English language media reports markedly decreased during this stage, and fewer reports appeared in the media. The publicly communicated messages were marked by an emphasis on certainty: "It is the sprouts," declared Reinhard Burger, chief of the Robert Koch Institute ("German official," 2011); and, "The discovery confirms our current warning against the consumption of bean sprouts. Enjoy lettuce, cucumbers and tomatoes. They are healthy for you," said Andrea's Hensel, president of the German Federal Risk Assessment Institute ("Deadly E. coli detected," 2011). Finally, on July 26, the Robert Koch Institute declared the outbreak officially over, with 52 deaths, and 4,321 having fallen ill from the infection ("Germany: E. coli outbreak is over," 2011).

The most notable public communication during this phase happened at the international level, as leaders, farmers, and others dealt with the economic and political repercussions of the outbreak. The European Commission, for example, released a public service announcement to assure the public that, "vegetables are good for you!" (Mayer-Hohdahl, 2011). There were also heated public exchanges with Russian officials, including Prime Minister Vladimir Putin, who expressed doubt that the outbreak was, indeed, finished: "We are appropriate [*sic*] pessimistic" ("Russian sanitary official," 2011). Responding to diplomatic pressure from the European Union to resume imports of vegetables, Putin replied: "Western producers for many years have got [*sic*] used to thinking of the Russian market as a fiefdom where they can do anything they want. An example is what is happening with vegetables" (Korshak, 2011). Furthermore, other media reports expressed concern over how Germany's response would affect its leading role in the European Union (Grech, 2011).

The post-crisis phase was marked by communication throughout the time period and across all agencies that clearly emphasized certainty. However, media reports indicated that these messages were received with a much higher level of skepticism than before. By the end of the crisis, public perception was poor enough that there were calls for some health officials to resign, as well as discussion about the need for reforming the public health apparatus in Germany.

CONCLUSION

The approach taken by Germany's health officials had mixed results. While officials were successful in warning the public about health risks, overly certain communication and culturally insensitive messages exacerbated the crisis. By examining positive, negative, and cultural impacts, key conclusions come into focus.

Positive Results of Navigation

In many ways, communication from German health officials achieved positive results. Most noticeably, the public did avoid lettuce, tomatoes, and cucumbers as directed by the various health ministries and institutes. The goal of crisis communication is to resolve or contain the ongoing threat to the public (Seeger, Sellnow, & Ulmer, 2003). These messages are effective only when the public takes the recommended actions. In this case, the precise source of the outbreak was not immediately known, but scientists knew that certain vegetables potentially carried the deadly disease. Avoiding these vegetables, therefore, was a logical step toward reducing the risk of further contamination.

News reports showed that the public did, in fact, heed this advice. The public's reaction to the advisory against these vegetables was clear. Reports revealed plummeting demand for vegetables, both in Germany and across Europe ("E. coli outbreak in Europe," 2011). For example, a high profile church event in the city of Dresden, attended by 120,000 people, decided against serving raw vegetables altogether: "I noticed that there were no raw vegetables, which I found calming," one attendee was quoted as saying. Another participant said: "I've thought about what I can eat and what I can risk. Yesterday I noticed someone saying: 'yuck, there's lettuce on top of this'" (Rising, 2011). In this sense, the public's reaction to the crisis was ideal.

Another positive result of the government's response was a well-informed public. German health officials communicated quickly and consistently, providing the public with daily information updates. During this time, spokespersons from various agencies involved in the crisis communicated directly to the public, rather than funneling information through a single source. While this led to some confusion, it did afford the public (and the media) a transparent view of the response. Eventually, the source of the contamination was communicated correctly to the German public.

Negative Results of Navigation

Despite the frequency and transparency with which health officials approached the German public, there were many negative results stemming from the navigation of the crisis. The most noticeable impact was economic: The public began to avoid all produce, not just the types advised against by public health officials (Kanter & Dempsey, 2011). The economic damages caused by this reaction soon became the driving force behind much of the public dialogue about the outbreak. For example, as health officials warned against various types of produce, some in the agriculture industry attacked the response as unnecessary or unfounded. Spanish farmers who had been accused of producing contaminated cucumbers staged protests across Spain as they threw away produce they could no longer sell because of the public's fear of contamination ("E. coli outbreak in Europe," 2011). This public display soon escalated as the Spanish government stepped in to demand an apology from Germany for mistakenly attributing the source of the E. coli to Spanish cucumbers. Moreover, the Spanish approached the European Union for compensation of over €200 billion ("E. coli outbreak in Europe," 2011). Meanwhile, Russia and many other countries banned vegetables imported from Europe, dealing yet another financial blow to farmers. These negative economic developments dominated the news cycle during the crisis and post-crisis phases.

Too much certainty in communication during the early stages of the crisis (before sprouts were definitively confirmed as the source of the outbreak) contributed not only to painful economic impacts, but also negatively affected the government's credibility. With each new and promising development, health officials began to communicate with certainty and confidence, only to be proven wrong. In this case, an excess of certainty, in fact, led to increased *uncertainty* among the public. During this time period, there were many accusations that the German food safety system was broken, as it seemed that each new development was a surprise to the very organizations that were responsible for knowing the facts in order to protect the public. Thus, by appearing overconfident and emphasizing certainty in their communication with the public, German health officials eroded the public's trust in their government's ability to protect them.

Throughout the crisis, there was evidence that the governmental responses were fragmented. As the focus of the crisis shifted (i.e., from cucumbers to uncertainty to sprouts and so on), each of the various health agencies communicated as separate entities. Sometimes, messages contradicted those put out by other agencies. As just one example of many, the Hamburg ministry of health communicated that it was closing in on the source ("E. coli 'Sproutbreak,'" 2011) while the RKI would say only that the investigation could take weeks ("E. coli mystery intensifies," 2011). These conflicting statements devolved to placing blame. After an official from another agency accused the other for being slow to recognize the beginning of the outbreak, an official from the RKI responded that, figuring out, "where the outbreak comes from—and also making sure that the contaminated food comes off the market—is the duty of the [states]" (Stevens, 2011). These public disagreements and contradictory statements regarding the progress of the investigation painted an unclear picture for the public.

Sometimes, the lack of uncertainty in the public messages was a result of the way they were crafted. Uncertainty was, in fact, present in many messages; but the sentiment was commonly cut from quotations, particularly if it was not at the beginning of the sentence. Sentences beginning with statements of uncertainty were more effective at communicating that uncertainty to the public. This is because uncertainty was often phrased in the form of a qualifying remark, not as a central component of the message. These qualifying remarks were often paraphrased or cut altogether from the reports; while the more certain, definitive elements of the message were quoted directly.

News reports from June 5 provide a salient example of this tendency. On this date, Gert Lindermann, Agriculture Minister for the state of Lower Saxony, was widely quoted in the media. Some news reports directly quoted portions of his statement, focusing on those remarks that expressed certainty in the new developments of the investigation. For example, the *International Business Times* quoted Lindermann: "a connection has been found involving all the main outbreak," and also quoted his advice to "not eat any bean sprouts right now" ("Bean sprouts 'Connection,'" 2011). The portions of his statement that expressed uncertainty were paraphrased, such as his note that the final lab results would be available on Monday, and that there was no definitive proof so far ("Bean sprouts 'Connection,'" 2011). Other media reports that day omitted these portions of the message. For example, the *Guardian* of June 5 reported that officials had identified bean sprouts as a likely source, with no reference to pending test results. Furthermore, the Associated Press quoted Lindermann as saying, "there were more and more indications in the last few hours that put the focus on this farm. . . . Many restaurants that suffered from any *E. coli* outbreak had the sprouts delivered" (Grieshaber & Skaro, 2011). These excerpts reflected the media's focus only on statements that portrayed certainty, while minimizing or altogether excluding statements or portions of statements that communicated ambiguity.

Cultural Impacts of Navigation

Existing cultural tensions contributed to a negative public dialogue that damaged the credibility of Germany's public health organizations. Spanish politicians and farmers were incensed that German officials were so quick to accuse them of supplying contaminated vegetables, especially when the source turned out to be disproven. In demonstrations and statements by politicians, some accused Germany of being xenophobic, and viewing Spain as a poor country of unsanitary peasant-run farms ("Germany: E. coli outbreak is over," 2011). German Chancellor Angela Merkel apologized to the Spanish at their request, but the economic and political ramifications of the accusations continued (Korshak, 2011).

Russia also capitalized on what they deemed an "incompetent" German response to the outbreak in order to reinforce existing political tension between the European Union and Russia ("Russian sanitary official," 2011). Russian Prime Minister Vladimir Putin used the crisis as an opportunity to score political points, criticizing the European Union food safety system that Russia had been asked to adopt. The fact that German health officials had mistakenly identified a number of sources, retracting their statements each time, was used as evidence of a broken system ("Russia bans EU vegetables," 2011). The resulting adversarial dialogue prompted one Russian ambassador to coin the phrase "EUcoli" (Norman, 2011). In this case, existing cultural tensions were exacerbated because health officials' changing, sometimes contradictory, messages were used to underscore a political argument.

STRATEGIES FOR END USERS

The ten best practices of crisis communication provide a framework through which organizations can improve their communication with the public (Seeger, 2006). In the case of Germany's response to the *E. coli* outbreak, the most salient lessons are to account for uncertainty, collaborate and coordinate with credible sources, and be culturally sensitive when communicating risk. These key lessons stand out during Germany's response.

Account for Uncertainty

In its most basic form, risk is the absence of certainty (Sellnow et al., 2009). Any action contains an element of risk if there is any uncertainty regarding the results an action will produce. In reality, absolute certainty is a rare luxury. Uncertainty, therefore, is the "central variable" in the risk communication process (Palenchar & Heath, 2002, p. 131).

Making statements that attempt to dispel uncertainty during a crisis situation is not the best approach. Research suggests that effective risk communication involves some level of "ambiguity or uncertainty that will enable the organization both to communicate with their public and to emphasize the level of uncertainty they are experiencing at the time" (Ulmer, Sellnow, & Seeger, 2007, p. 43). In short, an "organization must be able to communicate what it knows at the time" of a crisis (Ulmer et al., 2007, p. 43). This type of response will give the public a better sense of security.

Absolute statements about a crisis should be avoided until all the facts have been gathered. An overly assuring statement made early in the crisis phase can create two problems. First, it can make the public think something is being covered up, because most people understand there is an innate uncertainty in crisis situations (Sellnow et al., 2009). In this case, German health officials spoke too soon, often releasing information that would later be proven inaccurate. Changing and conflicting communication from various agencies at different points in time caused public confusion, frustration, and uncertainty. Thus, this case study illustrates that, in the absence of definitive information, it is prudent to emphasize that uncertainty when communicating with the public.

This case study also suggests that statements of uncertainty need to be emphasized and given primacy in risk and crisis messages. Accurately delivering risk messages can pose a challenge. As the previous section discussed, media articles examined in this study showed a propensity to directly quote statements of certainty, while paraphrasing or omitting statements emphasizing uncertainty. This revelation suggests that risk communication messages should not only include certainty, but spokespersons should consider structuring the message so that it is impossible to omit appropriate statements reflecting elements of uncertainty. For example, it would be easy to omit the second half of the following sentence: "All indications lead us to believe that sprouts are the source of the contamination, but we have to wait for further tests to be sure." Instead, a spokesperson could instead craft a message in such a way that it would be difficult for the media to omit statements of uncertainty. For example, "we won't know until we get the test results, but it is possible that sprouts may be linked to the outbreak." The removal of the uncertainty from the second statement would be difficult without completely altering the message. The examples from this case study demonstrate the impact media can have by editing public statements, and what impact the inclusion or removal of uncertainty may have on perceptions of risk and crisis messages.

Collaborate and Coordinate

A second relevant best practice concerns how risk communicators interact with each other. When considering any risk, a number of organizations will likely serve as sources of information. Consistent messages can help develop a more coherent and effective public understanding of risks. Inconsistent messages, on the other hand, can lead to confusion and frustration.

This case study shows the consequences of failing to fully collaborate and coordinate among relevant agencies. If partnerships are established in the pre-crisis phase, officials are better able to come together in order to manage resources and coordinate communication when a crisis develops. Looking back at this outbreak, it was clear that the state ministries of health operated independently of each other and independent from the RKI. Even though these government agencies were undoubtedly working together on the investigations, the public communication was seemingly uncoordinated. As a result, citizens received conflicting information about the nature of the crisis.

The lack of collaboration and coordination among officials and agencies intensified this crisis. As the previous section outlined, the lack of coordination often created inconsistent, sometimes conflicting, messages, leading to a perceived lack of competence—one that politicians in Spain, Russia, and elsewhere used to gain political leverage. Spain demanded monetary compensation, while Russia used this example as an excuse to ban imports and question the European food safety apparatus. These political and economic impacts could have been mitigated by presenting a coordinated message that emphasized the inherent uncertainty of the situation.

Design Risk Messages to Be Culturally Sensitive

Finally, this case study illustrates the importance of designing risk messages to be culturally sensitive. Perceptions of risk are socially and culturally constructed, and can be expected to vary widely based on several factors (Sellnow et al., 2009). Moreover, specific characteristics of the audience influence the way messages are received and interpreted. In cases where risk messages will be communicated to more than one cultural group, such messages are often more effective when they are delivered by a respected member of that particular community. Individuals from within cultures have more credibility with the intended audiences and understand cultural nuances. For this reason, messages from outsiders are less likely to be effective and may even create mistrust (Littlefield, Cowden, Farah, McDonald, & Sellnow, 2006). Understanding the personal, community, and cultural influences on risk perception can enable communicators to adapt their messages to each particular audience in order to receive a desirable outcome. Working with a spokesperson from within the culture will help achieve the desired effect.

The culture-centered approach to risk communication can give voice to the fears, frustrations, and questions of a group. This was most apparent when German health officials blamed Spanish cucumbers for the outbreak. While Germans simply may have viewed this as useful information, many in Spain viewed the accusation as derogatory and xenophobic, sparking protests from farmers and politicians. This resentment added to existing political, economic, cultural tensions that existed from the two countries interactions stemming from the European Union's economic crisis (Walker & Karnitschnig, 2010). German officials may have avoided much of this fallout simply by having a Spanish official present the initial findings that blamed Spanish grown cucumbers. Many Spanish farmers also felt that Germans were accusing them of unsanitary farming practices. A culture-centered approach when crafting the initial message would have taken this into consideration in order to mitigate any damage to the farmers' businesses and reputations.

The German *E. coli* outbreak presented unique challenges for the officials charged with responding to the crisis. This situation illustrated the importance of incorporating uncertainty into risk and crisis messages. Furthermore, it demonstrated that taking a culturally sensitive approach is key to navigating any crisis effectively. Communicators can limit negative outcomes by taking these factors into account when responding to a crisis.

REFERENCES

Bean sprouts "Connection" in E. coli outbreak. (2011, June 5). *International Business Times*.

Bronst, S. (2011, June 3). Germany: E. coli outbreak "stabilising." *Mail & Guardian*.

Brown, J. (2011, June 1). Cucumbers in clear—so what is causing deadly E. coli outbreak? *The Independent*.

Cheng, M., & Baetz, J. (2011, June 7). Experts: Time running out to solve E. coli mystery. Associated Press Financial Wire.

Cooper, B. (2011, August 5). German E. coli outbreak: After the outbreak the learning begins. *Just-Food*.

Crossland, D. (2011, June 7). Crises like the E. coli outbreak require central management. *Spiegel Online International*.

Cucumbers blamed for deadly Germany E. coli outbreak. (2011, May 26). Agence France Presse.

Deadly E. coli detected on bean sprouts for the first time. (2011, June 10). Xinhua General News Service.

Dempsey, J. (2011, June 7). First sprout farm samples test negative for E. coli; officials in Germany cite "very difficult" search for source of contamination. *International Herald Tribune*, p. 7.

E. coli mystery intensifies, Germany says bean sprouts are not to be blamed. (2011, June 7). *Asian News International*.

E. coli "Sproutbreak" kills 22. (2011, June 6). *Daily Record*, p. 2.

E. coli outbreak in Europe kills 16. (2011, June 1). *International Business Times News*.

Gale, J. (2011, June 4). Cow manure likely to blame for European E. coli outbreak; killed 19 people. *National Post*, p. A17.

German official: Sprouts source of E. coli. (2011, June 10). *United Press International*.

Germany probes sprouts as killer bacteria source. (2011, June 6). Agence France Presse.

Germany says its initial E. coli sample tests on sprouts negative. (2011, June 6). Xinhua General News Service.

Germany sees a sharp upswing in dangerous intestinal infections. (2011, May 24). *Deutsche Welle*.

Germany: E. coli outbreak is over. (2011, July 27). Associated Press.

Germany: E. coli outbreak is over. (2011, July 26). Associated Press.

Grech, H. (2011, June 13). E. coli problem under control, says EU health commissioner. *McClatchy-Tribune Business News*.

Grieshaber, K., & Skaro, T. (2011, June 6). Germany: Sprouts likely cause of E. coli outbreak. *The Daily Star*.

Hackenbroch, V., Shafy, S., & Thadeusz, F. (2011, May 31). The hunt for the source of Germany's E. coli outbreak. *Spiegel Online International*.

Hallinan, C. (2011, April 27). Europe's crisis and the pain in Spain. *Foreign Policy in Focus*.

Kanter, J., & Dempsey, J. (2011, June 2). E. U. seeks to defuse fears over E. coli; source remains mystery, but bloc opposes a ban on produce for now. *International Herald Tribune*, p. 1.

Kelsey, E. (2011, May 31). Contaminated vegetables kill 14; more than 300 seriously ill in Germany, officials worry the worst is to come. *Vancouver Sun*, p. B4.

Killer E. coli combines common toxin with rare "glue." (2011, June 3). *International Business Times News*.

Korshak, S. (2011, June 23). Putin: Europe can't think of Russia as a "fiefdom" for food exports. *McClatchy-Tribune Business News*.

Littlefield, R., Cowden, K., Farah, F., McDonald, L., & Sellnow, T. (2006). *Ten tips for risk and crisis communicators when working and conducting research with Native and new Americans*. Fargo, ND: Institute for Regional Studies.

Littlefield, R., Farrell, L., Beauchamp, K., & Rathnasinghe, S. (2012). Maintaining relationships with the public: Applications of relational dialectics theory in crisis communication. *National Communication Association*. Orlando, FL.

Mayer-Hohdahl, A. (2011, July 19). Vegetables are good for you, EU insists in post-E coli campaign. *McClatchy-Tribune Business News*.

Norman, L. (2011, June 8). E. coli row could overshadow EU-Russia summit. *Wall Street Journal*.

Outbreak of E. coli foodborne illness in Germany. (2011, May 26). *States News Service*.

Palenchar, M. J., & Heath, R. L. (2002). Terrorism and industrial chemical production: A new era of risk communication. *Communication Research Reports*, 22(1), 59–67.

Pidd Berlin, H. (2011, May 27). Germany: E. coli deaths lead to Spanish cucumber ban. *The Guardian*, p. 32.

Rising, D. (2011, June 3). Germany: E. coli patients continue to rise. Associated Press.

Russia bans EU vegetables over E. coli, EU protests. (2011, June 2). Saudi Press Agency.

Russian sanitary official skeptical about reports on end of E. coli outbreak. (2011, July 27). *Daily News Bulletin.*

Seeger, M. (2006). Best practices in crisis communication: An expert panel process. *Journal of Applied Communication Research, 34*(3), 232–244.

Seeger, M. W., Sellnow, T. L., & Ulmer, R. R. (2003). *Communication and organizational crisis.* Westport, CT: Praeger.

Sellnow, T. L., & Ulmer, R. R. (2004). Ambiguity as an inherent factor in organizational crisis communication. In D. P. Miller & R. L. Heath (Eds.), *Responding to crisis: A rhetorical approach to crisis communication* (pp. 251–262). Mahwah, NJ: Lawrence Erlbaum Associates.

Sellnow, T. L., Ulmer, R., Seeger, M., & Littlefield, R. (2009). *Effective risk communication: A message-centered approach.* New York: Springer.

Stevens, L. (2011, June 10). Germany: Sprouts to blame for outbreak. *Wall Street Journal.*

Trauner, S., Frey, A., & Kusidlo, S. (2011, May 23). Potentially fatal strain of E. coli spreading in Germany. *McClatchy-Tribune Business News.*

Ulmer, R. R., Sellnow, T. L., & Seeger, M. W. (2007). *Effective crisis communication: Moving from crisis to opportunity.* Thousand Oaks, CA: Sage.

Walker, M., & Karnitschnig, M. (2010, November 26). Europeans clash on bailout—EU officials propose doubling $588 billion fund, but Germany spurns idea. *Wall Street Journal*, p. A1.

Weick, K. (1995). *Sensemaking in organizations.* Thousand Oaks, CA: Sage.

Wendel, M., & Wegener, B. (2011, May 24). First death in Germany as super-bacterium spreads. *McClatchy-Tribune Business News.*

Chapter Five

The Tension of Organizational Interest

China's 2008 Melamine Milk Crisis

Tara B. Freed and Robert S. Littlefield

Economic adulteration is, "[a] deliberate substitution or addition of harmful ingredients in food and drugs," used to increase perceived product value and/ or reduce the cost of production (FDA, 2011, p. 1). Economic adulteration is an intentional, self-serving activity where the organization benefits at the cost of detrimental effects to consumers. In the past ten years China has been linked to numerous economic adulteration cases, including: methanol tainted wine in 2004, fraudulently labeled glycerin in 2006, the melamine crisis in pet food in 2007, toxic Herapin blood thinner in 2008, and adulterated and brand forgery of wine in 2010 (FDA, 2011). Arguably, one of China's most devastating cases was the melamine milk crisis in 2008 where close to 300,000 infants became ill and six infants died due to adulterated milk.

Gale and Hu (2009) explained, "Historically low consumption of milk in China reflected the scarcity of pasture, hay and cattle in densely-populated regions . . . [and] was consumed mainly by infants and elderly people" (p. 2). However, in the late 1990s, China's dairy sector rose dramatically, "[from] just over 1 million metric tons in 1980 to over 35 million metric tons in 2007" (p. 2). As demand grew for raw milk supplies, so did the competition among companies and the incentive to adulterate their milk products. To increase volume, companies added water to the milk supply. But, when the diluted milk failed to pass protein testing, deceitful companies added melamine and other "protein powders." As explained by the World Health Organization (2012):

> Companies using the milk for further production (e.g., of powdered infant formula) normally check the protein level through a test measuring nitrogen content. The addition of melamine [a chemical rich in nitrogen] increases the nitrogen content of the milk and therefore its apparent protein content. (para. 3)

Melamine is most commonly used in plastics, adhesives, countertops, dish-ware, and whiteboards. When ingested by humans, melamine can cause bladder stones, kidney stones, kidney failure, cancer, or even death (WHO, 2012).

China's 2008 melamine milk crisis is an excellent example of how the dialectical tension of self-serving versus other-serving is used to construct messages during a crisis situation. Understanding the issues involved in this case is useful for decision-makers when developing and communicating effective messages in response to a crisis. The remainder of this chapter presents the cultural context of this crisis, specifically examining how Confucianism values affected China's response to the crisis; the dialectical tension of self-serving versus other-serving as the central concept and theoretical underpinning of this case; two research questions requiring further inquiry; a detailed timeline of the pre-crisis, crisis, and post-crisis phases; the method for this case study, with a discussion of the results and analysis; and finally, a conclusion and strategies for end users.

CULTURAL CONTEXT

The cultural context of China's 2008 melamine crisis had an impact on how and why the Chinese people and authorities responded the way they did. The first influential factor, and a basis for understanding the overall response to this crisis, was China's pervasive Confucianism ideology (Tsao, 2011). Confucianism is a code of ethics that promotes a love for humanity, reverence for human relationships, and conduct conducive to a harmonious society. Sitaram's (1995) list of eastern society characteristics underscores this Confucianism ideology. Key values include a respect for authority and hierarchical systems; the importance of brotherhood, gratefulness and loyalty to family, and respect for elders; collective responsibility and cooperation; and sacredness of the land.

These values play an important role in how eastern societies, specifically China deal with conflict. Augsburger (1992) focused on conflict mediation across cultures and revealed that, "the traditional Chinese model of conflict resolution is based on saving face for both parties in dispute" (p. 95). Unfortunately, this type of face-saving often leads to confrontation avoidance instead of conflict resolution. A second influential factor in the cultural context of this crisis was the vulnerability of those hurt by the adulterated product. The tainted milk powder was used in infant formula, sickening 294,000 infants, and killing six (Fan, 2008). A third factor in the cultural context of this crisis was the impact of its spillover beyond China; in that a New Zealand-based company was part owner of the Sanlu, the entity responsible for the adultera-tion. The adulterated infant formula from Sanlu also was shipped to and sold in countries across Asia. A final influential factor was the coincidental and confounding timing of the melamine crisis and the 2008 Summer Olympic Games. Beijing hosted the Games of the XXIX Olympiad from August 8–24; and events were viewed by 4.7 billion worldwide (Martineau, 2008). Ironi-cally, China's Olympic motto, One World One Dream, was an expression meant to convey harmony and peace; core concepts of the Chinese people and their Confucianism ideology (BOC, n.d.).

THEORETICAL UNDERPINNINGS

Littlefield, Farrell, Beauchamp, and Rathnasinghe (2012) used Baxter's rela-tional dialectics theory to explore dialectical tensions decision-makers experi-ence when constructing crisis messages. Baxter's (1990) relational dialectics theory suggested the following:

> The centrality of the process concept mandates a theoretical domain focused on developmental change. Such change is the result of the struggle and tension of contradiction from a dialectical perspective. A contradiction is present whenever two tendencies or forces are interdependent (the dialectical principle of unity) yet mutually negate one another (the dialectical principle of negation). (p. 70)

Overall, "when facing the dialectical tensions associated with construct-ing crisis messages, oppositional positions must exist in order for response strategies to be implemented" (Littlefield et al., 2012, p. 5). Littlefield et al. identified seven dialectical tensions inherent in the decision-making process when constructing crisis messages, including: timeliness (immediate vs. delayed), amount of information (open vs. closed), confidence of informa-tion (certain vs. uncertain), interest (other-serving vs. self-serving), level of responsibility (owning vs. disowning), voice(s) in media (one vs. multiple), and emotional connection (sensitive vs. insensitive). The basis for this chap-ter is the specific dialectical tension of interest, or other-serving versus self-serving. Other-serving versus self-serving reflects a focus on prioritizing one interest over the other. Littlefield et al. defined other-serving as occurring when, "[the] message reflects a focus on prioritizing the interests of others, over the organization's interests"; and self-serving as, "reflect[ing] a focus of prioritizing the organization's interest, over the interest of others" (Littlefield et al., 2012, Table 2).

Economic adulteration—a common phenomenon studied by food safety experts—is an example of self-serving activity. In 2007, melamine-laced pet food imported from China killed dozens of dogs and sickened thousands more ("Melamine . . . ," 2011). In 2008, nearly 150 people died and hundreds more become ill because of a toxic contaminant that was added to Herapin, a common blood thinner (USP, 2012). In cases like these, researchers focused on the harm caused to public health, impact on the public's confidence for safe food and medical products, economic consequences after major recalls, and/or halts to production (FDA, 2011). These specific cases also caused the U.S. Food and Drug Administration to call for better coordination to enhance efforts to address adulteration and protect public health (FDA, 2011). Missing from these earlier studies was a focus on the dialectal tensions experienced by the decision-makers when these crises occurred.

RESEARCH QUESTIONS

Economic adulteration can lead to devastating effects, including severe illness, long lasting complications, or death. Although the impacts of intentional contamination have been idenified, no study has examined economic adulteration in relation to relational dialectics theory, specifically the dialectical tension of self-serving versus other-serving. This study explores that gap by revealing how the dialectical tension of interest confronted decision-makers in China's 2008 melamine milk crisis. This chapter also demonstrates how the cultural context affected the resolution of the crisis. With that, two research questions are posed:

RQ1:   How did Sanlu and Chinese officials navigate the dialectical tension of interest (self-serving vs. other-serving) when dealing with melamine milk crisis?

RQ2:   How did the context of the Chinese culture affect the ability of Sanlu and Chinese officials to resolve the crisis?

METHOD

A case study approach was used to identify how the dialectical tension of interest (other-serving vs. self-serving) was at play during China's 2008 melamine milk crisis. The database for this study included domestic and international news sources. Domestic news sources included the *New York Times, Time* magazine, and the *Washington Post*; international news sources included *Xinhua News*, BBC News, New Zealand Stuff, the *Sydney Herald*, and Radio Free Asia. Within days of the crisis becoming public, the Chinese Propaganda Department "swiftly deleted" Internet discussions and

Table 5.1. Crisis Timeline for 2008 Melamine Crisis in China

Phase One—Pre-Crisis—General Notice of Problem

March, 2008	Sanlu received complaints about its baby milk powder. An investigation was performed, the problem was confirmed, but neither the government nor public were notified of the possible contamination.
August 2, 2008	Fonterra, a New Zealand-based company and part owner of Sanlu, became aware of the adulterated milk during a Sanlu board meeting. Fonterra urged Sanlu for a full public recall.
September 5, 2008	Fonterra alerted Helen Clark, New Zealand prime minister, of the adulterated milk in Beijing.
September 8, 2008	Clark bypassed Chinese government and authorities and ordered that the Beijing public be notified of the adulterated milk.
September 10, 2008	A Chinese news agency, Xinhua, reported that fourteen infants had developed kidney stones in the western province of Gansu. Other cases were reported around China.

Phase Two—Crisis—Direct Connection between Problem and Source

September 11, 2008	Jian Guangzhou, reporter for the *Oriental Morning Press*, was the first journalist to make public the direct connection between the adulterated milk and the Sanlu group.
September 12, 2008	Sanlu admitted its milk powder was contaminated with melamine.
September 13, 2008	Production at Sanlu stopped with nineteen people arrested.
September 15, 2008	Bejing confirmed two infant deaths. Sanlu VP apologized for the harm caused to infants and their families.
September 22, 2008	Head of China's quality watchdog resigned. Wen Jiabao, respected Chinese government leader, expressed guilt and apologized for crisis. Current impact included 53,000 ill infants and four infant deaths.
September 23, 2008	Countries across Asia began to test milk/dairy products from China or pull them from shelves.
October 23, 2008	Six more people arrested in connection to the adulterated milk.
November 14 & 18, 2008	The U.S. issued an "import alert" for Chinese-made food products. The Chinese government allowed the U.S. to station officials in three cities to ensure safety of Chinese exports.
December 2008	Sanlu filed for bankruptcy. Trials began for Sanlu workers/executives connected to the adulterated milk.

Phase Three—Post Crisis (Point Where Crisis is Resolved)

December 27, 2008	300,000 people affected by the adulterated milk were compensated by dairy firms involved in the scandal.
January 2, 2009	Twenty-two companies connected to the scandal sent a text message to millions of Chinese cell phone users apologizing for the adulterated milk scandal.
January 2009	China reported a total of 260,000 children falling ill due to the melamine milk crisis, six infants died. In total, sixty people were arrested and twenty-one sentences were handed out (ranging from two death sentences to compensation). Parents of the first baby who died received $29,000 from Sanlu; 213 families whose children were affected or died from the adulterated milk petitioned the Supreme Court for higher levels of compensation.

(BBC, 2008; Elegant, 2008; Toy, 2008; RFA, 2008)

other public forums being used to publicize the adulterated milk (Elegant, 2008); therefore, only comments reported in domestic or international news sources before being deleted from the Web were used in this study. The database from which examples were drawn was published between September 15, 2008 and February 2, 2009.

The data were deductively coded using Littlefield et al.'s (2012) dialectical tension continuum of interest, looking for messages representing self-serving versus other-serving interests.

Coding for other-serving messages included content where the focus was on, "prioritizing the interest of 'others,' over the organization's interests" (Littlefield et al., 2012, p. 36). An example of other-serving interest coding was: "Our highest priority is doing what is best for the public." Coding criteria for self-serving messages involved a message where the focus was on, "prioritizing the organization's interest, over the interest of others" (Littlefield, 2012, p. 36). An example of self-serving interest coding was: "Our goal is to ensure our organization retains our normal sales/profits . . ."

Table 5.2.   Coding Criteria for Focus on Interest

Continuum Anchor	Dialectical Tension	Continuum Anchor	Coding Criteria and Coding Examples
Other-Serving ♦———♦	Interest	Self-Serving	♦ Other-Serving: Message reflects a focus on prioritizing the interest of "others," over the organization's interests. (For example: *"Acting in the best interest of the public is our highest priority."*) ♦ Self-Serving: Message reflects a focus on prioritizing the organization's interest, over the interest of others. (For example: *"Our goal is to resume operations as soon as possible . . ."*)

RESULTS AND ANALYSIS

The results of this case study of China's 2008 melamine milk crisis are reported in three phases: Phase 1, the pre-crisis, begins when there is a general notice of a problem; phase 2, the crisis, begins when a direct connection between the problem and the source is identified; and the final post-crisis phase, begins when the crisis is resolved, positively or negatively. For each phase, Sanlu's and the government's statements and actions were analyzed using the dialectical tension coding criteria for interest, ranging along the continuum of self-serving to other-serving.

Phase 1: Pre-Crisis

The pre-crisis phase revealed examples of both other-serving and self-serving messages and actions. In March of 2008, Sanlu received its first complaints about the quality of its baby milk powder. Sanlu responded to these complaints with its own product investigation, confirming the problem and recalling some of the tainted products. The company, however, failed to issue any statements about its responsibility or recommendations for consumers to take action ("Sanlu apologizes . . . ," 2008). Fonterra, a New Zealand-based dairy cooperative and part owner of Sanlu, responded very differently to the complaints. Fonterra became aware of the adulterated milk on August 2, 2008, during a Sanlu board meeting. That day, Fonterra ordered Sanlu to make a full public recall. After a month of inaction by Sanlu, on September 5, 2008, Fonterra notified New Zealand Prime Minister Helen Clark of the potential crisis; three days later she ordered that the Beijing public be notified, bypassing Chinese authorities (Toy, 2008). Clark blamed the six-week cover-up on Chinese officials, saying that Fonterra urged for a public recall but, "Local authorities in China would not do it . . . . I think the first inclination was to try and put a towel over it and deal with it without an official recall" (Toy, 2008, para. 7).

Internet forums blamed the Chinese government and Sanlu for the cover-up suggesting they, "had colluded to cover up the scandal because of central Government pressure to ensure that no bad news blighted China's hosting of the Olympics" (Toy, 2008, para. 8). Fu Jianfeng, editor of the respected Chinese newspaper, *Southern Weekend*, reported that his newspaper knew of the potential crisis in July. As reported in *The Australian*, Fu blogged: "As a news editor, I was deeply concerned because I sensed that this was going to be a huge public health disaster. But I could not send any reporters out to investigate. Therefore, I harboured a deep sense of guilt and defeat at the time" ("China accused . . . ," 2008, para. 9–10). Fu's blog post has since been removed. The first public notification of a potential problem was finally reported on September 10, 2008, when the Chinese news agency Xinhua reported that fourteen infants had developed kidney stones in the western province of Gansu and other cases were being reported around China (BBC, 2008).

Phase 2: Crisis

The crisis stage—when a direct connection between the problem and the source was identified—began on September 11, 2008, when Jian Guangzhou, a Chinese journalist, publicly connected the adulterated milk to Sanlu (BBC, 2010; RFA, 2008). The next day, Sanlu admitted its connection to the adulterated milk powder stating that, "it had found in its self-check that some of its baby milk powder products were contaminated" ("Sanlu admits . . . ," 2008, para. 1). The company also promised to recall baby milk products produced before August 6, 2008. The recall was the company's first other-serving message during the crisis. On September 13, production at Sanlu stopped and nineteen people were arrested in connection with the crisis.

As the crisis became public, the Chinese Propaganda Department took action and ordered the media to "tone down" coverage of the crisis, warned lawyers to drop plans of suits on behalf of the victims and their families, and deleted Internet discussion of the disaster (Elegant, 2008, para. 4). The second other-serving message came three days later; after Beijing confirmed two infant deaths, Sanlu's vice president Zhang Zhenling apologized at a news briefing on September 15, 2008. As quoted by *Xinhua News*, Zhenling stated:

> The serious safety accident of the Sanlu formula milk powder for infants has caused severe harm to many sickened babies and their families. We feel really sad about this . . . . Sanlu Group expresses its most sincere apology to you . . . . We solemnly declare we will recall all the infant milk powder produced prior to August 6. And for those produced after that date, we will also make a recall if consumers have doubts and worries. ("Sanlu admits . . . ," 2008, para. 1–3)

This message was other-serving because it publicly announced the recall and also gave power to the people when additional recalls were offered, if deemed necessary by consumers. However, some parents didn't accept these messages. Zhang Zaihua, a parent of a nineteen-month-old girl who fell ill due to the tainted milk, felt this crisis was due to a collective moral corruption, stating: "'Enough with the hindsight. . . . Where were all those supervisors before this whole thing happened?'" (Elegant, 2008, para. 5).

On September 22, the head of China's quality watchdog agency resigned as Beijing reported that the tainted milk had left 53,000 infants ill and four dead. That same day, Wen Jiabao, the most popular figure in China's leadership, commented that, "he felt 'extremely guilty' about the poisoned milk products that have killed four babies and sickened tens of thousands, adding, 'I sincerely apologize to all of you'" (Elegant, 2008, para. 1). Again, although the actions and statements seemed to show other-serving behavior, parents were still angered. Ling, whose baby became ill due to the adulterated milk opined: "They hurt our babies, and in our hearts we can never be healed again. We are very disappointed" (RFA, 2008, para. 6–7).

On September 23, countries across Asia began testing milk/dairy products from China or began to completely pull them from shelves. One month later, on October 23, six more people were arrested in connection to the crisis. In November, the Chinese government allowed the U.S. to station officials in three cities to ensure safety of Chinese exports; this action came four days after the U.S. issued an "import alert" on November 14 for Chinese-made food products. This other-serving action was the only one reported where the Chinese officials dealt with the crisis as both a domestic and international problem. On December 2008, Sanlu filed for bankruptcy and trials began for Sanlu workers/executives connected to the crisis.

Phase 3: Post-Crisis

This stage of post-crisis began when the crisis was resolved. On December 27, 2008, the 300,000 known people affected by the adulterated milk were compensated by dairy farms involved in the scandal (BBC, 2010). One parent angered by the amount stated: "I spent nearly 20,000 yuan taking care of my son, and the government only compensated me with 2,000" (Barboza, 2009, para. 10). On January 2, 2009, millions of mobile phone users in China received a mass text from twenty-two of the companies connected to the scandal. The two-part text included an apology, acceptance of responsibility, and a promise that it would not happen again. The message also noted victims were being compensated. The text ended with best wishes for the New Year (Elegant, 2009). Some believed the text was merely, "a PR exercise or an attempt by the government to damp down public anger over the issue" (Elegent, 2009, para. 1). Throughout the month of January, sixty people were arrested and twenty-one sentences handed out, ranging from compensation to two death sentences. Again, parents were angered. Liu Donglin, a parent of a two-year-old boy who suffered kidney stones from the tainted milk said, "They are just scapegoats. The ones who should take the responsibility are the government, like the quality supervision bureau and the Health Ministry" (Barboza, 2009, para. 10).

CONCLUSIONS

A relational approach to crisis communication ultimately provides a way to examine message construction in crisis situations. This study examined the dialectical tension of interest (self-serving vs. other-serving) in China's 2008 melamine milk crisis. It also explored how the cultural context affected the resolution of the crisis. This case study revealed that while Sanlu and Chinese government officials used both self-serving and other-serving messages and actions during the crisis, overwhelmingly, most of the other-serving messages and acts were viewed as disingenuous and few perceived positive results.

During the pre-crisis phase, Sanlu and Chinese government officials displayed only self-serving behaviors. For example, Sanlu was notified of problems with its powered milk supply in March of 2008, but did not publicly admit connection and fault until September 12, 2008—seven months later. The decision by Chinese officials government to wait to address the crisis until after the Olympic Games also led to negative feelings from the public. Fonterra, a New Zealand-based company, was the force behind the public recall. In addition, New Zealand's prime minister publically blamed the Chinese government for the deadly delay in action.

During the crisis phase, Sanlu and government officials responded with many other-serving messages and acts; but few were seen as genuine and many were seen as too little, too late. For example, Sanlu admitted fault for the tainted milk and made a public recall, but the announcement and recall came after thousands of infants were already sickened and two infant deaths were confirmed. During the crisis phase, the Sanlu vice president and a respected Chinese leader gave apologies to the public. However, due to the continuous string of Chinese crises, and the after-the-fact manner of the apology, this other-serving message did not hold much weight and appeared meaningless to many. In actuality, the Chinese government made many arrests; most involved the dairy farmers and the middle-men in the operation. Although this may be regarded as other-serving, the public felt that those charged were merely scapegoats, and the government itself should have been the entity held accountable (Barboza, 2009). On the domestic front, Chinese authorities allowed the U.S. to station officials in three cities to ensure the safety of exports. This was one of the few positive actions taken by the government in reaction to the crisis.

Finally, in the post-crisis phase, more negative reactions to Sanlu and the government's response to the crisis appeared. On January 2, 2009, millions of Chinese cell phone users received a text message from the companies involved in the crisis. Although this text allowed the companies to apologize and promise that a similar transgression would not occur again, it was seen by many as a public relations gesture from the government that didn't address the needed changes in China's quality control (Elegant, 2009). Arrests also were made in the post-crisis phase. However, these were not seen as bringing justice, as much as they were viewed as the government's attempt to blame others for the crisis.

The cultural impacts were apparent in every stage of the adulterated milk crisis. The traditional Chinese model of saving face during conflict resolution was clearly seen in the pre-crisis stage. Although the Beijing government was notified of the adulterated milk, it did not take action or notify the public for fear of receiving negative press while China hosted the Olympic Games. In the crisis stage, face-saving strategies occurred during the court sessions of the persons/companies involved in the scandal. As reported by Barboza (2009), "Beijing even attempted to detain or block parents from traveling to Shijiazhuang to listen to the verdicts. Foreign journalists have also been barred from attending some of the court sessions" (para. 14).

Finally, China's Confucianism ideals upholding authority and hierarchical systems were observed in the post-crisis stage. During this stage, the government simply apologized and returned to business as usual. Although many Chinese believed a structural reform was needed, "The top leadership can't get over their anxiety that any structural reform will mean the end of one-party rule" (Elegant, 2008, para. 7).

STRATEGIES FOR END USERS

The National Center for Food Protection and Defense (NCFPD) developed ten best practices that organizations should use when communicating with the public during crises. The intent of these practices was to help reduce or prevent negative effects of a crisis situation (Seeger, 2006). Strategic planning involves three best practices: pre-event planning and preparedness, collaboration and coordination with credible sources, and the acceptance of uncertainty and ambiguity. Proactive strategies include: partnerships with the public; listening to the public's concerns; and demonstrating honesty, candor, and openness. Strategic responses include: the need to meet the media's needs, communication with compassion, concern and empathy, and communicating meaningful actions. Finally, process approach and policy development includes the final best practice of viewing risk and crisis communicating as an ongoing process.

In this case, it is unknown how much strategic planning occurred within Sanlu. Proactive strategies appeared to be missing completely. Sanlu may have had a better outcome if its officials would have connected with the public, listened to their concerns, and been open and honest about the crisis situation. For example, the government and Sanlu ignored the crisis and needed actions until the Olympic Games were over. If they would have presented this information during the Olympics, it may have been in the news for one cycle, but much of the attention may have been avoided. An early response to the crisis also would have made later strategies more effective and appear genuine. Sanlu's strategic response was lacking. Foreign media were barred from court happenings, local media outlets given little information, and the public was not provided any meaningful course of action. Finally, the Beijing government did not appear to use the final best practice; as the public perceived the government's apology and return to business as usual as insincere, and a failure to make crisis communication an ongoing process.

Overall, by taking a dialectical approach to message construction in a crisis situation much can be learned. This case study showed how the dialectical approach of interest can fall within a continuum of self-serving versus other-serving messages. China's 2008 melamine milk crisis showed how important upfront, other-serving messages are, and how vital they are for later strategies to be effective.

REFERENCES

Augsburger, D. W. (1992). *Conflict mediation across cultures: Pathways and patterns.* Louisville, KY: Westminster/John Knox Press.

Barboza, D. (2009, February 2). Death sentence given in Chinese milk scandal. *New York Times.* Retrieved from http://www.nytimes.com.

Beijing Organization Committee (BOC). (n.d.). *"One World One Dream."* Retrieved from http://en.beijing2008.cn.

Baxter, L. A. (1990). Dialectical contradictions in relationship development. *Journal of Social and Personal Relationships 7,* 69–88.

BBC News. (2010, January 25). *Timeline: China milk scandal.* Retrieved from http://news.bbc.co.uk.

China accused of Olympic milk cover-up. (2008, October 1). *The Australian.* Retrieved from http://theaustralian.com.au

Elegant, S. (2008, September 23). China's poisoned-milk scandal: Is sorry enough? *Time.* Retrieved from http://world.time.com.

Elegant, S. (2009, January 2). Milk powder mass mailing. *Time.* Retrieved from http://world.time.com.

Fan, M. (2008, December 3). 6 Chinese infants died in milk crisis. *Washington Post.* Retrieved from http://www.washingtonpost.com.

Food and Drug Administration (FDA). (2011). *Better coordination could enhance efforts to address economic adulteration and protect the public health* (GAO Publication No. GAO-12-40). Washington, DC: U.S. Government Printing Office.

Gale, F., & Hu, D. (2009). Supply chain issues in China's milk adulteration incident. Contributed paper prepared for International Association of Agricultural Economists' Conference, Beijing, China.

Littlefield, R. S., Farrell, L. C., Beauchamp, K., & Rathnasinghe, S. (2012). Maintaining relationships with the public: Applications of relational dialectics theory in crisis situations. Paper presented at the meeting of the 2012 National Communication Association, Orlando, Florida.

Martineau, J. (2008, September 5). *2 out of 3 people worldwide watched 2008 Beijing Olympics.* Retrieved from http://www.nowpublic.com.

Melamine—Tainted baby formula scandal. (2011, March 4). *New York Times.* Retrieved from http://topics.nytimes.com.

Radio Free Asia (RFA). (2008, September 23). *Uproar over China milk scandal.* Retrieved from http://www.rfa.org/english/news/china/.

Sanlu admits contamination of baby milk powder products. (2008, September 12). *Xinhua News*. Retrieved from http://www.china.org.cn.

Sanlu apologizes for milk powder contamination. (2008, September 16). *Xinhua News*. Retrieved from http://www.china.org.cn.

Seeger, M. W. (2006). Best practices in crisis communication: An expert panel process. *Journal of Applied Communication Research, 34*(3), 232–244.

Sitaram, K. S. (1995). *Communication and culture: A worldview.* New York: Mc-Graw Hill.

Toy, M. (2008, September 16). Sabotage claim in milk powder scandal. *The Sydney Herald.* Retrieved from http://www.smh.com.au.

Tsao, R. (2011). Harmony: The essence of China's culture of peace. *Chinese American Forum, 27*(2), 17–21.

U.S. Pharmacopeial (USP). (2012). *Responding to a crisis: Herapin.* Retrieved from http://www.usp.org.

World Health Organization (WHO). (2012). *Questions and answers on melamine.* Retrieved from http://www.who.int.

Zhang, S., & Prosser, M. H. (2012). Globalization, Asian modernity, values, and Chinese civil society. *China Media Research, 8*(2), 18–25.

Chapter Six

The Tension of Taking Responsibility

The Failings of Del Bueno in the Queso Fresco Crisis

Jessica Rick and Robert S. Littlefield

During any crisis situation, companies are forced to navigate the fine line between owning and disowning primary responsibility for the crisis. A major tenant of current corporate social responsibility focuses on the awareness of a company to take the responsibility for a negative situation in order to better society. A company may want to take responsibility in a situation but may not be capable because many factors determine the ability of a company to respond. Del Bueno went through a series of recalls of their cheese products in 2010 and 2011 and eventually closed in 2012. Throughout the crisis, Del Bueno was unable to take full ownership of its actions due to financial constraints, but it was legally forced to take ownership of the food contaminations in its plant, thereby taking primary responsibility for the situation.

This case study follows the Del Bueno crisis from 2010 into early 2012 specifically looking at when and how the company either took ownership of its actions or dis-owned the Listeria contaminations happening in its processing facility. This chapter begins with an explanation of the cultural context of the situation to increase awareness about the implications of working within a crisis involving cultural differences. Second, a brief overview of image restoration and corporate social responsibility provides the standards and expectations of businesses during crisis situations. Next, a general timeline illustrates the phases of the Del Bueno crisis. Following a brief methodology section, the results and analysis of the case explain how Del Bueno initially showed dis-ownership but eventually, was forced to take ownership of the crisis. Finally, the general conclusions of the case and strategies for future crises are recommended to help governmental agencies and corporations learn from the Del Bueno food safety crisis.

CULTURAL CONTEXT

Del Bueno was a small family-owned company located in Grandview, Washington, specializing in the production of soft, Mexican cheeses. Queso fresco (or fresh cheese) is the most common Mexican-style cheese produced and is often used to top salads, beans, and rice as well as being served as the filling in stuffed chilies, enchiladas, or quesadillas (Wise Geek, 2012). The Del Bueno product recalls specifically affected the Hispanic communities in Washington and Oregon, introducing a cultural component to the crisis. People of Hispanic or Latino descent are the largest minority group in both Washington and Oregon, comprising approximately 12 percent of the population in each state (U.S. Census, 2010). A minority group was affected by this food safety crisis with the dominant culture and government dictating regulations for Del Bueno to follow for producing a safer food product. Within this co-cultural context, two important considerations need to be addressed: food and language.

Food is an important aspect of a culture (Harris & Moran, 1991). Culture dictates what foods people eat, how the food is prepared, and how people eat the food (i.e., chopsticks, hands, utensils). In this case, a prominent aspect of cultural context involves how food is normally prepared. Queso fresco is traditionally made from raw milk. However, in the United States, manufacturers must use pasteurized milk due to the bacteria found in unpasteurized dairy products. This cultural difference played an important role in how the Del Bueno crisis transpired.

Another cultural aspect to this case was the language used in the media and by the government during the crisis. Language is an important indicator of power between cultural groups. In the U.S., English is not an official language, but most governmental agencies, media, and consumer transactions take place in English. In contrast, one in five Americans uses a language other than English at home; more specifically, Spanish (U.S. Census, 2007). The reliance on Spanish as the primary language can leave individuals vulnerable if they are not conversational in and able to read English. (For more information about language, power, and culture, see Sadri and Flammia, 2011.)

THEORETICAL UNDERPINNINGS

The dialectical tension (Baxter, 1990) of interest in this case study was the level of responsibility an organization or business takes for causing the crisis situation. In other words, does the organization take responsibility or disown it, blaming the crisis on some other entity (Littlefield, Farrell, Beauchamp & Rathnasinghe, 2012). Benoit's theory of image restoration focuses on the strategies used by companies to deflect or deny responsibility in order to protect their images (Benoit, 1995). These strategies include denial, evading responsibility, reducing offensiveness, corrective action, and mortification. Two of these strategies are particularly relevant to responsibility. The strategy of denial includes simple denial, or stipulating that the act did not occur, and shifting blame, occurring when an organization blames another entity for the crisis situation. Organizations also can use the strategy of evading responsibility when the crisis is blamed on an accident, good intentions (i.e., when the act that started the crisis was meant well), and defeasibility (i.e., when the crisis occurs due to the lack of information or ability to make the changes necessary). All of these strategies are used to help an organization repair its image during and after a crisis.

Another area where level of responsibility has been studied is within the corporate social responsibility research (CSR). CSR is broadly defined as how companies manage business processes to produce an overall positive impact on society (Carroll, 2008, Hunnicutt, 2009). Legal corporate responsibility encompasses the responsibility by companies to comply with the laws set in place by national and local governments (Hunnicutt, 2009). Of relevance to the Del Bueno crisis is the fact that the U.S. Food and Drug Administration (FDA) mandates a variety of laws and food processing policies ensuring safe products for consumer consumption. Along with these laws, every culture has moral and ethical standards by which businesses must abide. It is important to note what is considered *socially responsible* is determined by the economic, ethical, and moral expectations of a society at a given point in time (Carroll, 2008). Therefore, these expectations may change in different cultures or co-cultures functioning within one larger culture. In the United States, society has placed an expectation on organizations to own—or take responsibility for—a crisis situation and change their procedures to be in line with the current laws.

RESEARCH QUESTIONS

Given the cultural differences between the dominant culture and the minority Hispanic culture, along with the theoretical aspects of image restoration and corporate social responsibility at play in the dialectal tension of showing ownership/dis-ownership, the following research questions emerged:

RQ1: How did Del Bueno navigate the dialectical tension of level of responsibility when dealing with the Queso Fresco crisis?

RQ2: How did the cultural context of the Hispanic community affect the ability of Del Bueno to resolve the crisis?

Table 6.1.   Timeline of the Del Bueno Crisis

Timeline

Phase One—Pre-Crisis	
Pre-2010	FDA and WSDA started routine inspections of the Del Bueno manufacturing plant.
April 2010	During one of the routine inspections, Listeria monocytogenes were found in the plant. Del Bueno was notified and recalled all packages of Queso Fresco due to the potential contamination with Listeria in the final product.
November 2010	After another inspection, Listeria monocytogenes were found again in the plant and in samples of finished products. Del Bueno was notified and recalled all packages of Queso Fresco, Queso Panela, Requeson Mexican Style Ricotta Cheese, and Queso Enchilado Dry Cheese due to the potential contamination of Listeria in their finished products.
Phase Two—Crisis	
April 1, 2011	Del Bueno received a warning letter from the FDA stipulating the need for an action plan to reduce the likelihood of Listeria in Del Bueno's products.
September 2011	WSDA held another inspection and found Listeria monocytogenes in both the plant and finished products. WSDA notified Del Bueno and the company recalled the 16 oz. package of Queso Fresco due to the potential of Listeria contamination in the finished product.
March 2012	FDA closed the Del Bueno manufacturing plant due to repeated outbreaks of Listeria.
Phase Three—Post-Crisis	
April 2, 2012	Del Bueno and the FDA entered consent decree to keep Del Bueno's products off of the market until they are proven safe.
April 9, 2012	Del Bueno declared the intent to close all operations.

METHOD

Database

A case study approach of the Del Bueno crisis was used to examine the dialectical tension of level of responsibility perceived by the company and media coverage of the crisis. The original website search of *"Del Bueno"* produced thousands of results in Spanish due to the common use of the phrase "del bueno"; therefore, the search was refined to *"Del Bueno recall."* A search on the *Lexis-Nexis* database limited to *"Del Bueno recall"* yielded thirty-five articles; however, many of these articles were duplicates. These articles ranged in date from April 6, 2010 to April 10, 2012. These articles included press releases from the FDA, news outlet stories, and websites covering the recalls. An additional five articles were retrieved from blogs and websites.

Coding Procedures

Following established coding procedures (Littlefield, et al., 2012), statements and actions of Del Bueno were analyzed on a continuum to determine the level of responsibility the company took during the crisis. Owning actions and statements involved the company claiming full responsibility for the crisis. For example: "this was our fault." Whereas, *disowning* actions and statements include statements such as "we are not at fault."

Table 6.2. Coding Criteria for Organizational Responsibility

Continuum Anchor	Dialectical Tension	Continuum Anchor	Coding Criteria and Coding Examples
Owning	Level of Responsibility for Crisis ♦———♦	Disowning	♦ Owning: Organization claims full responsibility for the crisis. (For example: *"This was our fault . . ."*) ♦ Disowning: Organization disowns full responsibility for crisis. (For example: *"We are not at fault . . ."*)

Analysis of the data revealed interactions of the dialectical tension of owning versus disowning during three phases: Pre-Crisis, Crisis, and Post-Crisis. Phase one, or the Pre-Crisis Phase, is the first data collection point, beginning prior the first recall of Del Bueno's products. The Crisis Phase, the second data collection point, started when the FDA sent a warning letter to Del Bueno. During the third data collection point and phase three of the crisis, or the Post-Crisis Phase, the data were collected to determine whether the business was able resume operations after the crisis. The results of the case study follow.

RESULTS AND ANALYSIS

Pre-Crisis Phase

Starting in 2009, the Washington State Department of Agriculture (WSDA) started conducting routine checks of the Del Bueno processing plant. During one of the routine inspections, the WSDA found contaminated cheese during sampling; and later linked a Listeria illness back to Del Bueno's Queso Fresco (Flynn, 2010). The company was notified on April 6, 2010, and worked with the FDA to recall all 16-ounce packages of its product, Queso Fresco. On April 7, the recall was extended to all Queso Fresco products (FDA, 2010).

The FDA conducted another routine inspection of the plant in October 2010 and discovered Listeria monocytogenes in both the plant and in finished products. Del Bueno received the notice November 10, 2010, and on November 17, 2010, Del Bueno voluntarily announced a recall of all packages of Queso Fresco, Queso Panela, Requeson Mexican Style Ricotta Cheese and Queso Enchilado Dry Cheese due to the possibility of a Listeria contamination (Targeted News Service, 2010). No illnesses were reported with this recall (Associated Press, 2010).

Between these recalls, Del Bueno did not take ownership of the Listeria crisis. The company made no public statements regarding the recalls, but as the saying goes, "actions speak louder than words." In this case, it was the inaction of Del Bueno that spoke louder than their words. The owners had the opportunity to take responsibility and change their processing procedures to make a safer cheese for the public's consumption. However, they did not make the necessary changes after the first recall and had to recall their product again for Listeria contamination. If appropriate responsibility would have been taken, the second recall may not have been issued. The company's inaction demonstrated an inherent denial of responsibility.

Crisis Phase

Phase two started on April 1, 2011, when Del Bueno received a warning letter from the FDA reminding Del Bueno it was, "responsible for ensuring that [their] processing plant operates in compliance with . . . applicable regulations. [The FDA] may take further action if you [Del Bueno] do not promptly correct these violations" (FDA, 2011). The letter cited the October 2010 visit to the processing facility and finished samples from early November 2010 as instances where Listeria monocytogenes were found in Del Bueno's products; specifically asserting, "the presence of a persistent strain of L. monocytogenes in [the] facility . . . demonstrates that sanitation efforts were inadequate to remove this organism" (FDA, 2011). This letter is the first step taken by the government to force ownership on Del Bueno for the Listeria contamination crisis.

For the third time, the WSDA found Listeria monocytogenes in the Del Bueno processing plant during a routine check. Del Bueno received the notice on September 16, 2011, and recalled their 16-ounce packages of Queso Fresco (News Desk, 2011). Despite the warning from the FDA in April 2011, Del Bueno still had not taken responsibility of the situation. The owners had not made the necessary changes stipulated by the government to make a healthy and safe product. In March 2012, the FDA closed the Del Bueno processing plant due to the repeated Listeria outbreaks and the lack of ownership to make the necessary changes and rectify the situation.

Post-Crisis Phase

Phase three started when the FDA and Del Bueno entered a consent decree issued by the Washington state courts on April 2, 2012, despite Del Bueno, "disputing the FDA's findings that there were chronic [Listeria] problems" (Robinson, 2012). This agreement stipulated that Del Bueno must keep its products off the market until they can prove they make a safe product for the general public. Among other things, Del Bueno was charged with ensuring the following compliance strategies: (1) "Hire an independent laboratory to collect and analyze samples for the presence of Listeria; (2) retain an independent sanitation expert; (3) develop a program to control Listeria for all employees in both English and Spanish; and (4) destroy all food items currently in the facility" (Rothschild, 2012). The courts forced Del Bueno to take full responsibility for the Listeria contaminations and mandated the owners to make changes before the reopening its doors.

On April 9, 2012, Jesus Rodriguez, the son of the owner, stated: "We were planning to go ahead and do what they asked us to do. But I think my dad's last decision was just to close. . . . He doesn't think we can make it through. We don't have enough money to start back up again" (Robinson, 2012). This statement pointed to the fact that Del Bueno was unable to financially afford to take full responsibility and ownership of its actions, and the Queso Fresco crisis. Despite this lack of resources, the courts legally forced Del Bueno to take ownership of its actions during the crisis. As of February 2014, Del Bueno has not reopened its doors.

CONCLUSION

Throughout phases one and two of the crisis, Del Bueno did not take ownership of its actions or ownership of the Listeria monocytogenes found in the plant and in its finished Del Bueno products. Using one of Benoit's (1995) image restoration strategies, defeasibility, the company was not able to financially afford the mandated changes necessary to take full ownership of the Listeria contamination. It was not until the courts legally forced Del Bueno to take responsibility that ownership was placed on the company. There were no public statements or quotations in the data indicating whether or not the company wanted to take responsibility for the crisis sooner. The only indication made public was the fact that Del Bueno did not make changes to its processing procedures despite the FDA mandate. During phase three, the public learned that Del Bueno was not able to financially afford the ownership of their past behaviors when the owner stepped out and made a public statement. Therefore, it is important to realize that other factors played a role in the ability of the organization to take full responsibility of its actions, regardless of societal expectations.

Corporate social responsibility emphasizes that businesses have a responsibility to society (Carroll, 1999; Hunnicutt, 2009). This responsibility lines up with the current economic, ethical, and moral expectations of a society. In the United States, these obligations are designed to ensure the health and welfare of the general public. However, these expectations represent the dominate culture's ethical and moral standards; not necessarily the standards of the minority consumers of Del Bueno. Queso fresco is traditionally made from raw milk, but the legal standards in the United States dictated the use of pasteurized milk. Del Bueno was in touch with the users of its queso fresco, who represented the minority co-culture; whereas, the WSDA and FDA represented the government of the dominant culture and norms. In the United States, food safety and corporate responsibility expectations represent the dominant norms and these tend to supercede all other cultural norms. The traditional custom of making queso fresco meets the ethical and moral standards of the Mexican culture, not the cultural expectations of the United States dominant culture. In the present crisis, the members of the dominant culture dictated how members of a minority culture should prepare their food products. The government set certain ethical and legal standards to ensure the safety of the consumers, but the imposed rules and expectations on Del Bueno went against the traditional process of making queso fresco from unpasteurized milk. In the end, the dominant culture's food preparation norms forced the minority's processing plant to close because it was not up to the dominant culture's ethical and legal standards of public safety, regardless of the minority's norms in food preparation.

Language also played an important role in this case. The owners, as well as a majority of their workers, were Hispanic. As part of the consent decree, Del Bueno was required to provide all safety procedures in both English and Spanish to its workers. While in this stage of the crisis, the government recognized the need for multilingual procedures; during phases one and two, multilingual information uniformly was not available. During the pre-crisis and crisis stages, a large number of affected individuals were not aware of the safety concerns about consuming this particular brand of cheese. Thus, the language barrier was an important factor in this case; especially for the targeted market.

Throughout the Del Bueno crisis, several barriers influenced the outcome of the recall crisis as well as the ability of Del Bueno to take ownership of its actions. First, Del Bueno was not able to financially afford taking responsibility for the Listeria contamination and making the necessary changes to stay in business. Second, the Hispanic food processing norms of preparing queso fresco were in conflict with the dominant U.S. cultural, legal, and moral standards. Finally, the language barrier proved to be a factor in the case due to the large number of Hispanic customers.

STRATEGIES FOR END USERS

The Del Bueno crisis ended with the company being forced to close by the FDA; and it has not reopened its doors since. Fortunately, other companies and governmental agencies can learn from Del Bueno and incorporate different practices during a crisis situation. There are four main lessons for government agencies and businesses to realize: First, it is important to realize other factors play a role in determining a company's ownership; next, companies and governmental agencies need to recognize cultural differences; third, language barriers influence a crisis situation; and finally, companies need to be prepared for unexpected situations and realize that crisis communication is an ongoing process.

Ability of Ownership

The first takeaway from the Del Bueno crisis involved the ability of a business to take responsibility for a crisis situation. Current American ethical and moral expectations assume that a company will try to resolve an issue if public health is at risk (Grace & Cohen, 2005). However, not all companies are able to make the necessary changes. Del Bueno stated during phase three that it was not financially able to change the cheese making process to meet the FDA standards. Therefore, Del Bueno was not fiscally able to take ownership and rectify the situation. Governmental entities should realize that not all companies can make the necessary changes in a short amount of time. Changing major processes takes time and governmental agencies should consider offering assistance to businesses to help them meet the necessary legal and health standards to resume normal operations rather than forcing heavy sanctions in a short amount of time, in effect killing the company.

Food Is Cultural

Another important lesson from the Del Bueno case is the importance of understanding there can be a cultural component to food recalls. Per cultural norms, food is prepared and eaten in traditional ways. For dairy products in the United States, this includes using pasteurized milk. However, in Mexico, queso fresco is made from raw, unpasteurized milk. This cultural norm is in direct odds with the dominant American norm pertaining to the way food is prepared. Particularly in co-cultural contexts, governmental agencies should realize that the way food is prepared and consumed is culturally determined. Therefore, when dealing with a crisis involving ethnic foods, it is not necessarily easy for a business to change the ways the food is prepared without having to change the nature of the food itself. The legally mandated changes may not be feasible for the foods a particular company produces. Rather than closing facilities, the government should (a) work with companies to make the product safer for public consumption as well as (b) inform the public (in multiple languages) about the dangers of eating a particular food product. Consumers are more likely to make educated decisions about the consumption of particular food products if the dangers of particular foods are explained and their cultural norms included in the discussion.

Language Barrier

Another cultural component for both businesses and governmental agencies to recognize is that language is a barrier in crisis situations. For the Del Bueno recalls, a majority of the customers were of Hispanic descent and a number of those were unable to read English. Therefore, much of the information released by the company and FDA in English only did not reach the essential audience. Governmental agencies need to ensure all groups are getting the proper information. This includes publishing reports in multiple languages and in multiple outlets—both mainstream media and co-culture media outlets—to ensure the public is getting the necessary information regarding a crisis.

Best Practices

Planning Is Essential

The next two strategies pertain to business professionals working in the field. Seeger (2006) created a list of best practices for organizations experiencing crises to help them communicate with their publics. Littlefield et al. (2012), proposed a relationship between these best practices and the continuums of the relational dialectics theory. Two best practices relate to the tension of ownership and dis-ownership: pre-event planning and preparedness, and viewing risk and crisis communication as an ongoing process. In terms of the first best practice, pre-event planning and preparedness, organizations must have a crisis plan in place. In terms of organizational responsibility, plans should be in place and resources should be allocated to be prepared for a crisis. If something were to happen, it will be easier for the organization to navigate the ownership/dis-ownership tension with a plan in place.

New Information Changes Things

For the second best practice, organizations need to realize that risk and crisis communication is an ongoing process. New information changes the perception of the business, the level of ownership, and how an organization might manage a crisis situation. For Del Bueno, the managers did not take ownership during the first recall. After another recall, they still did not take the ownership of the Listeria contaminations. In fact, they did not take ownership until they were forced to do so by the Washington state courts. Del Bueno was able to disown one Listeria contamination originally, but after three recalls and a warning letter they were unable to keep disowning the situation. New information and new cases changed Del Bueno's ability to disown the problems happening in its processing plant. Organizations need to accept that new cases and recall situations will force them to take ownership of the situation and make the necessary innovations to address the problem. Crisis communication is an ongoing process and new information initiates and influences that process.

The Del Bueno recall crisis was an interesting case examining the relational tension of level of responsibility. Originally, the company did not take any ownership in the Listeria contaminations; but, through legal and ethical obligations brought on by the government and dominant culture, the company was forced into ownership of the crisis. In this case study, four take away points were found to help organizations and governments deal with future crises in cultural contexts:

- Several factors played a role in determining whether or not this organization took responsibility of crises. These included, but were not limited to, legal factors, financial factors, cultural norms, and ethical standards.

In situations where dominant and subordinate cultures co-exist, there are several cultural and power dynamics that can effect a crisis situation:

- Organizations and governments need to publish materials in multiple languages and in multiple media outlets to reach the optimal audience in culturally sensitive situations.
- Organizations need to plan for events ahead of time and be prepared for situations that may arise.
- Organizations need to realize that risk and crisis communication as an ongoing process and new information changes that conversation.

REFERENCES

Associated Press. (2010, November 18). Product recalls: Cheese. Newswire.

Baxter, L. A. (1990). Dialectical contradictions in relationship development. *Journal of Social and Personal Relationships, 7*, 69–88.

Benoit, W. L. (1995). *Accounts, excuses and apologies: A theory of image restoration strategies*. Albany, NY: State University Press.

Carroll, A. B. (1999). Corporate social responsibility: Evolution of a definitional construct. *Business & Society, 38*, 268–295.

Carroll, A. B. (2008). A history of corporate social responsibility: Concepts and practices. In A. Crane, A. McWilliams, D. Matten, J. Moon, & D. S. Siegel (Eds.), *The Oxford handbook of corporate social responsibility* (pp. 19–46). New York: Oxford University Press.

FDA. (2010, April 7). Del Bueno amends recall of queso fresco cheese because of possible health risk [Press Release]. Retrieved from http://www.fda.gov/Safety/Recalls/ArchiveRecalls/2010/ucm207627.htm

FDA. (2011, April 1). Warning letter. Retrieved from http://www.fda.gov/ICECI/EnforcementActions/WarningLetters/2011/ucm253517.htm

Flynn, D. (2010, April 8). Queso fresco recalled by WA cheese maker. Retrieved from http://www.foodsafetynews.com/2010/04/listeria-hits-third-washington-cheese-maker/

Grace, D., & Cohen, S. (2005). *Business ethics: Problems and cases* (3rd ed.). Melbourne: Oxford University Press.

Harris, P. R., & Moran, R. T. (1991). *Managing cultural differences* (3rd ed.). Houston: Gulf Publishing Company.

Hunnicutt, S. (2009). *Corporate social responsibility: Opposing viewpoints*. Farmington Hills, MI: Greenhaven Press.

Littlefield, R. S., Farrell, L., Beauchamp, K. A., & Rathnasinghe, S. (2012). Maintaining relationships with the public: Applications of relational dialectics theory in crisis situations. Paper presented at the National Communication Association Conference, Orlando, Florida.

News Desk. (2001, September 18). Washington's Del Bueno recalls cheese again. *Food Safety News*. Retrieved from www.foodsafetynews.com

Robinson, J. (2012, April 9). FDA shuts down Del Bueno cheese producer. Retrieved from http://www.npr.org/templates/story/story.php?storyId=150318804

Rothschild, M. (2012, April 9). Listeria problem shuts down a Washington cheese company. Retrieved from http://www.foodsafetynews.com/2012/04/listeria-problems-shuts-down-a-washington-cheese-company/

Sadri, H. A., & Flammia, M. (2011). *Intercultural communication: A new approach to international relations and global challenges*. New York: Continuum International Publishing Group.

Seeger, M. W. (2006). Best practices in crisis communication: An expert panel process. *Journal of Applied Communication Research, 34*(3), 232–244.

Targeted News Service. (2010, November 17). Del Bueno recalls cheese because of possible health risk.

U.S. Census. (2007). Language use in the United States: 2007. Retrieved from http://www.census.gov/hhes/socdemo/language/data/acs/ACS-12.pdf

U.S. Census. (2010). Quick facts. Retrieved from http://quickfacts.census.gov/qfd/index.html

Wise Geek. (2012). What is queso fresco? Retrieved from http://www.wisegeek.com/what-is-queso-fresco.htm

Chapter Seven

The Tension of Controlling the Narrative

Construing and Mis-Construing Risk Messages

Elizabeth L. Petrun

November 6, 2012, became a milestone for those working toward policy supporting the *Dinner Party* in America. In California, a natural and organic food movement yielded a petition with enough signatures to introduce Proposition 37 (known as Prop 37) to state voters. The policy read: "government scientists have stated that the artificial insertion of DNA into plants, a technique unique to genetic engineering, can cause a variety of significant problems with plant foods" (Bowen, 2012, p. 110). In response to these "significant problems," Proposition 37 would require the mandatory labeling of foods produced through genetic engineering (GE) in order to monitor the health effects of GE products (Bowen, 2012).

By adding this proposition to the ballot, California residents brought their concern over GE food to debate at the state level. This case offers an example that identifies the tension that arises for a government agency or large corporation when counternarratives are introduced to misconstrue the original narratives that had been depicted as scientifically accurate. The regulatory voice on the GE food narrative comes from the U.S. Food and Drug Administration (FDA), which maintains that GE food is compositionally equivalent to products bred in traditional ways. This chapter illustrates how the U.S. FDA *lost control of its narrative*, which prompted a national debate over the legitimacy of GE foods in addition to the viability of the FDA as a regulatory agency.

The Prop 37 debate ushered two competing narratives to the forefront for consumers: one established narrative supporting the scientific evidence that GE foods are safe, the other counternarrative claimed these scientific assertions are unsubstantiated. Scherer and Juanillo (2003) identified the fundamental nature of such competing narratives by claiming, "what is really at issue is whether we have sufficient space to understand and talk about the specific prisms through which both scientists/experts and the public view risk'' (p. 222). Heath (2004) noted that through the consideration of such competing narratives, "the world and people's actions reflect a logic that explains what happens, why it happens, who makes it happen, when it happens, and how people should respond to these events" (p. 171). As such, the construal of facts and evidence in narratives around controversial issues has a profound influence on public sentiment and, ultimately, public policy. The tension between these competing narratives illustrates the importance of maintaining control over a narrative, and demonstrates the tangible consequences when multiple viewpoints manifest and compete with one another.

This chapter analyzes the competing narratives surrounding Prop 37, focusing particularly on how the two narratives construed the evidence associated with GE foods. The cultural context, theoretical underpinnings, and discussion of the tensions associated with controlling the narrative provide a backdrop for practical applications for decision-makers.

CULTURAL CONTEXT

The Prop 37 case is an example of tension between the scientific and lay community. Thus, the cultural context is undergirded with a conflict between those who believe that nature can be controlled to improve the quality and quantity of the food supply through genetic engineering versus those who believe that humans should not attempt to control the food supply by artificial genetically engineered means. This difference in worldview provides a fundamental point of conflict and for those who agree with the latter perspective, and results in counter narratives to refute the dominant scientific view. These conflicting narratives contribute to the tensions experienced by decision-makers within federal and multinational organizations as they attempt to control the narrative in their favor.

Laypersons, or those who do not have a background or expertise in a topic, piece together constructions of risk from a variety of familiar resources. Due to the inherent uncertainty associated with risk and risk communication, those with competing points of view can generate distinct narratives (Palenchar & Heath, 2002). In highly controversial or politicized cases, "the narrative of one group can be a counterstatement and perhaps a corrective to the narrative of another group" (Heath, 2004, p. 173). Consumers, voters, and other stakeholders are left to construe meaning from these competing perspectives. In the case of Prop 37, supporters pieced together their information from grass roots campaigns and activist leaders, beginning with Pamm Larry.

Pamm Larry, a fifty-six-year-old activist, started the campaign to get Prop 37 to the ballot. A former grower of organic herbs and flowers, Larry personally spearheaded the effort to require product labeling (Jargon & Berry, 2012). The proclaimed farmer, midwife, businesswoman, and "gutsy grandmother" of three quit her day job to educate herself about GMOs and ballot initiatives to tackle the United States' "modern day food system(s)," which she believed were responsible for unhealthy and artificial food (Spiegelman, 2012, para. 7). She began the process by driving to local festivals and farmers' markets to collect enough signatures to propel Prop 37 forward.

Those who opposed Prop 37 based their narratives on the scientific conclusions provided by the FDA. On May 29, 1992, the FDA published its statement, "Policy: Foods Derived from New Plant Varieties," constituting the founding document on GE food. In 1992, the FDA determined that, "[the] intended expression product or products present in foods derived from new plant varieties will typically be proteins or substances produced by the action of protein enzymes, such as carbohydrates and fats and oils." These substances, being already present in consumed foods, posed an "unlikely" safety concern and thus would not "warrant formal premarket review and approval by the FDA" (FDA, 1992).

While the FDA is the authority on GE foods, it is important to note the agency does not have a comparable spokesperson to Larry. In fact, the FDA does not comment on the merits or drawbacks of GE food, but rather continues to serve as an impartial regulatory authority. However, the persistence of competing narratives challenging the scientific narrative resulted in opposition to Prop 37.

Considering the cultural context of this case is essential to understanding the difficulty the opponents to Prop 37 had in controlling the non-scientific narrative. As Littlefield (2015) suggested: "To be successful with multiple publics, agencies and organizations cannot merely ignore or minimize the concerns of those who disagree. . . . Merely dismissing them as 'the crazies' because their arguments seem illogical or appear to manipulate the facts is ineffective" (p. 1). The impact of differing worldviews complicates the decision-making process for those seeking to control the risk narrative.

THEORETICAL UNDERPINNINGS

People "construe relevance and meaning from a given risk issue's myriad messages and relationships," to arrive at a decision (Sellnow, Ulmer, Seeger, & Littlefield, 2009, p. 8). To construe specifically means, "The public must infer meaning by assessing the importance and accuracy of the information and the authenticity of the source" (Sellnow et al., 2009, p. 8). Conversely, mis-construal occurs when laypersons incorrectly construct meaning. This misconstrued meaning affects decision-making processes, and in turn may impede others from arriving at the most ideal choice. Over time, construal and mis-construal may fuel competing interpretations, and eventually grander narratives, about an idea.

Events associated with strong feelings can overwhelm our judgment and bring people to erroneous conclusions (Rottenstreich & Hsee, 2001). When risk as emotion, or misunderstanding due to lack of evaluation or resources, overtakes risk as analysis, choices can become flawed or misguided. Further, research suggests that persons tasked with measuring risks are often in fact guided by their emotions (Slovic, Finucane, Peters, & MacGregor, 2002). Slovic, Finucane, Peters, & MacGregor (2004) elaborated that risk is actually best discussed in three categories, including "risk as feelings," "risk as analysis," and "risk as politics" (p. 311). Misconstruing a risk is a consequence associated with Slovic et al.'s (2004) assertion that risks can be interpreted first and foremost as "feeling," producing a different outcome than those using a "rational" approach to decision-making (p. 311).

Sinaceur, Heath, and Cole (2005) found that people enact both consequentialist decisions (when the costs and benefits of alternative choices are weighed) and cognitive decisions (when consequences are assessed non-emotionally and rationally) during risk deliberations. However, individuals may not always act rationally. In fact, Sinaceur et al. (2005) tested food-labeling alternatives in France and found that describing an animal disease with different terms can influence the vitality of the beef industry. For example, labeling risk as "mad cow" disease instead of "Bovine spongiform encephalopathy" (or BSE) evoked different components of the risk-decision-making process even though the terms described the same disease (Sinaceur et al., 2005, p. 247).

Managing the subjective construction of threat becomes important for organizations wishing to avoid mis-construal. As Sinaceur et al. (2005) discovered, terminology alone is enough to disrupt the vitality of the beef industry. Unnecessary disruptions to business can harm organizational legitimacy, growth, and increase the cost of product for end users. In these instances, it can be exceptionally important to maintain control of a food narrative.

Similar to the beef industry's fear of the term *mad cow disease*, vendors who rely on GE products worry that activist groups will falsely represent what is currently a safe process for cultivating food. As Rottenstreich and Hsee (2001) described, events associated with strong feelings can overwhelm judgment and produce erroneous conclusions. Consumers indicated that feelings about chemicals, for example, deterred them from buying and consuming certain foods (Petrun, Flood, Sellnow, Smith Edge, & Burns, 2015). However, chemicals in many instances perform positive functions like diminishing the likelihood of foodborne illness. Consumers though rarely investigate the necessity of chemicals in food and often perceive them as being fundamentally harmful (Petrun et al., 2015). This emotional push can overwhelm technical assessments of risk and allow irrationality into decision-making.

Food is a particularly powerful topic of discussion. If, for example, consumers truly believe that (1) GE food is harmful to them, and/or (2) they are being manipulated by unscrupulous organizations, they are likely to demand meaningful change. Unfortunately, the problem with this thinking is that little to no empirical evidence is available to suggest that more risk is associated with GE foods.

RESEARCH QUESTIONS

The challenge associated with construal and mis-construal is to understand what is missing or misinterpreted by the publics. Secondly, communicators need to determine the best way in which to reconcile this gap in information. In order to gain understanding of how losing control of a narrative impacts the ability to effectively resolve a crisis, the following research questions are proposed:

RQ1:   What was the pro-Prop 37 narrative, and how was it communicated?
RQ2:   What was the anti-Prop 37 narrative, and how was it communicated?
RQ3:   How did the cultural context of each narrative affect the ability of the respective groups to control the outcome of the 2012 proposition?

The following section includes a brief case description of GE food in the United States.

CRISIS TIMELINE

Case Background

GE food was introduced to U.S. markets in the 1990s, when farmers began using crops that were bred to repel pests and/or withstand herbicides. The FDA (2013a) defined genetic engineering as methodology used by scientists, "to introduce new traits or characteristics to an organism." The FDA (2013a) also noted in its primary definition a strategic choice to use the term genetically engineered instead of "genetically modified" (or Genetically Modified Organisms (GMOs) as the latter is "the more precise term."

Table 7.1.   Crisis Timeline of Proposition 37

1970s	First genetically engineered microorganism developed.
1986	U.S. federal government employs framework to manage biotechnology.
1990s	GE food introduced to U.S. markets.
1992	FDA releases Guidance to Industry for Foods Derived from New Plant Varieties.
Early 2012	Prop 37 enjoys popular support in California.
June 2012	American Medical Association agrees with FDA's labeling policy.
Oct. 2012	Prop 37 experiences decline in support.
Nov. 2012	Prop 37 rejected by California voters.
2013	Vermont first state to pass GE labeling legislation.
2013	Major distributors (Whole Foods and Kellogg's) impose guidelines requiring GE labeling by 2018.
2015	GE food labeling bills, amendments, and resolutions proposed in numerous states, Massachusetts, Hawaii, Florida, and Iowa.
2015	H.R. 1599, Safe and Accurate Food Labeling Act of 2015, introduced.

Since 1986, the U.S. federal government has employed a coordinated framework to manage agricultural biotechnology. The United States Department of Agriculture (USDA) (2013) described the broader term of biotechnology as the processes of, "breeding techniques that alter living organisms, or parts of organisms, to make or modify products; improve plants or animals; or develop microorganisms for specific agricultural uses." These processes are guided, tested, and approved by three agencies including the USDA's Animal and Plant Health Inspection Service (APHIS), the Environmental Protection Agency (EPA), and the Department of Health and Human Services' FDA. Currently, according to the Non-GMO Project, 93 percent of soy, 88 percent of field corn, 94 percent of cotton, and more than 90 percent of canola seed and sugar beets in the United States are genetically engineered (Beecher, 2013). Relatedly, these products are incorporated into other American made foods as ingredients, which disseminate GE products into thousands of finalized products available to consumers.

Prop 37 was touted as one of the first pieces of policy that would usher in a new era of food reform and governance in the United States. Pushing for labeling of products in the state would demand further attention from national regulators and industries. Products would also likely require substantive (e.g., costly) changes to comply with the state's new law. However, Prop 37 would not be the first time California enacted drastic policy changes in this manner.

The state's initiative process has been used by voters for decades, providing an avenue for a, "last- or first-ditch way for issues that politicians aren't yet ready to touch" to go to the public (Pollan, 2012, para. 2). Other attempts included the tax rebellion of the 1970s (Prop 13) and medical marijuana in the 1990s (Prop 215), which then proceeded to direct political discussions, including discussions in Washington, D.C. (Pollan, 2012, para. 2). Thus, passing Prop 37 could have impacted not only California voters, but also local, state, and national industries, governments, and regulatory bodies.

Earlier in 2012, polls showed that passing Prop 37 was strongly supported in the state (Walsh, 2012). Beginning in October, polls fluctuated to show narrower margins. While Prop 37 ultimately failed to pass with 52.9 percent voting against the mandate in comparison with 47.1 percent voting in favor of the legislation, this closely split initiative indicated significant support for both competing narratives (California Secretary of State, 2012).

The momentum did not subside following the referendum, and supporters of the initiative remain focused on altering content in the Farm Bill to encourage labeling systems of GE food. An activist group called "JustLabelIt" suggested in March 2013, that fourteen states were considering similar bills to Prop 37, including Washington, Iowa, Illinois, Minnesota, Vermont, New York, and Maryland (Leschin-Hoar, 2013).

In May 2013, Vermont's House of Representatives became the first state to pass a bill similar to Prop 37 that requires GE food to be labeled (Wilce, 2013). However, the state has yet to enforce the law. In addition to Vermont's success, certain retailers, including Whole Foods grocery store, have considered setting their own standards for GE food. Whole Foods is imposing a deadline for its suppliers to label GE foods by 2018 (Leschin-Hoar, 2013). Other companies like Kellogg's (a traditionally strong opponent of GE labeling) are now segmenting certain branches of their products to be GE free (including Kellogg's GoLean cereals and granola bars) (Leschin-Hoar, 2013).

In 2015, bill introductions, failures, and amendments have been ongoing in many states, including Maine, Connecticut, North Dakota, Michigan, Illinois, Massachusetts, Hawaii, Florida, and Iowa (Flynn, 2015). While activity seems to ebb and flow at the state level, many local lawmakers are focused on the outcome of the Safe and Accurate Food Labeling Act of 2015 in Washington, D.C.

METHOD

This analysis employs a case study method to provide, in rich detail, a description of how the narratives for and against GE labeling developed and interacted during the 2012 Prop 37 debate in California. The case study method is fitting for the analysis of competing narratives because it "allows investigators to retain the holistic and meaningful characteristics of real-life events" (Yin, 2003, p. 2).

Data Sources

In addition to reviewing the media coverage of the debate, this analysis focused on the organizational documents from the FDA and California Right to Know providing the competing narratives. First, organizational documents from FDA illuminated the regulatory agency's perspective on GE safety and legitimacy. FDA documents included: the Federal Food, Drug, and Cosmetic Act; the Statement of Policy–Foods Derived from New Plant Varieties; Completed Consultations on Bioengineered Foods; Guidance for Industry: Voluntary Labeling Indicating Whether Foods Have or Have Not Been Developed Using Bioengineering; Draft Guidance; and several FDA homepages that discuss GE foods. These FDA documents were selected for their presence in citations from newspapers and prominence in searching for GE information on the regulatory agency's website.

Press releases from the California-based "Right to Know" group provide insight into a pro-GE labeling group. California's Right to Know organization endorsed Prop 37 and was acknowledged by the state of California's voting materials for voters who wanted to receive more information on the issue. In total, fifty-one press releases were included for analysis (these fifty-one press releases included all organizational press releases posted online).

Information also was gleaned from interviews with Martina Newell-McGloughlin, director of University of Southern California's Biotechnology Research and Education Program, and Diana Reeves, president of GMO Free USA. McGloughlin and Reeves agreed to and completed interviews over the telephone. Interviews were confirmatory and explicated communication surrounding the labeling of GE food.

Coding Procedures

Using multiple sources of data provided for a robust understanding of competing narratives surrounding GE food. Consulting newspapers, organizational documents, and two organizational leaders offered perspectives on risk communication for both sides. The data were examined using the tension of control of the narrative, one of the seven tensions identified by Littlefield et al. (2012).

The source and material supporting and opposing Proposition 37 were identified during the coding process. The findings are presented in the following analysis.

Analysis

Even though Prop 37 failed to pass in California, the policy generated changes in both government and private industry. The next section details key

Table 7.2. Coding Criteria and Coding Examples

Continuum Anchor	Dialectical Tension	Continuum Anchor	Coding Criteria and Coding Examples
One	Voices In Media ♦————♦	Multiple	♦ One Voice: Organization maintains control of the messages/narratives in the media. (For example: *"This is the only pertinent information about this subject."*) ♦ Multiple: There are multiple voices in the media. (For example: *"There are several points of view with conflicting reports in the media about this subject."*)

arguments in narratives opposing and supporting Prop 37. In both narratives, the construal and mis-construal of scientific evidence is emphasized and discussed as it relates to the cultural context of each group.

THE SCIENTIFIC NARRATIVE OPPOSING PROPOSITION 37

From the perspective of the scientific community, compositionally, GE food is no different than non-GE food. Thus, the FDA's Federal Food, Drug, and Cosmetic Act mandated (in section 403) that food should not be misbranded or misleading–a stipulation that was needed to ensure the credibility and safety of products for consumers. Section 403, however, also applies to mislabeling products for benefits, increased nutritional quality, or other attributes. As the FDA finds GE food to be compositionally similar to traditional varieties, labeling GE food differently is at odds with the agencies' guiding operations.

The FDA's document entitled, "Guidance for Industry: Voluntary Labeling Indicating Whether Foods Have or Have Not Been Developed Using Bioengineering; Draft Guidance," explained that, "if a bioengineered food is significantly different from its traditional counterpart such that the common or unusual name no longer adequately describes the new food," the product's name would need to change (FDA, 2001). Since GE products are genetically similar to traditionally bred products, they must be treated the same as non-engineered food.

To date, the FDA has not commented on the public debate surrounding GE food. The agency has updated its website to include a new homepage that centralizes information about GE plants. FDA also compiled a document entitled, "FDA's Role in Regulating Safety of GE Foods," in addition to a "Questions and Answers on Food from Genetically Engineered Plants" (FDA, 2013b; FDA, 2013a). The document that discusses regulation and safety describes plant-breeding methodology, safety, and briefly mentions the organization's stance toward GE foods and labeling. Specifically relating to organizational views, the document states, "the agency neither supports GE plants based on their perceived benefits nor opposes them based on their perceived risks" (FDA, 2013b). The agency is most concerned that U.S. foods are "safe and otherwise in compliance with the FD+C Act and applicable regulations" (FDA, 2013b). FDA's frequently asked questions page covers ten common questions, ranging from "what is 'genetic engineering'" to "how is the safety of food from a genetically engineered plant evaluated?" (FDA, 2013a). Responses to questions are short and contain minimal jargon.

Based on the position established by the FDA, labeling GE food was viewed as unnecessary because humans have selectively bred and perpetuated desirable crops and animals for thousands of years (Ritter & Borenstein, 2010). This process, refined by gene engineering, "is a proven way to reduce disease, protect from insects and increase the food supply to curb world hunger" (Ritter & Borenstein, 2010, para. 12). Genetic engineering, unlike natural selection or breeding techniques, is more accurate and predictable than trying to control natural pollination or breeding livestock. Martina Newell-McGloughlin, director of the University of Southern California's Biotechnology Research and Education Program, noted: "genetic engineering is more precise and predictable, yet it is regulated up the wazoo" (Ritter & Borenstein, 2010, para. 20). In any respect, "all the food we eat, whether brussel sprouts or pork bellies, has been modified by mankind" (Specter, 2012, para. 3).

Unlike natural processes, GE foods have also been studied "hundreds of times over the past two decades, the National Academy of Sciences, the British Royal Academy, and scores of other scientific bodies have concluded they are no more dangerous than other foods" (Specter, 2012, para. 4). The American Medical Association (AMA) has said that GE crops "pose no new or different risks than any other crop, and there is no scientific reason to believe they would be any more risky" (Specter, 2012, para. 4). The problem then rests with the fact that arbitrary labeling would provide undue concern from consumers, leading them to avoid foods that contain ingredients that do no harm (Jargon & Berry, 2012). A Kraft foods representative said the measure "could disrupt [their] ability to meet consumer demand for [their] products, increase costs for California consumers and increase frivolous lawsuits against businesses" (Jargon & Berry, 2012, para. 14).

The effects of stripping the GE food industry of operational capacity by requiring labeling and other bans are serious. For example, Tomson (2010) wrote that U.S. sugar production could have been cut by 20 percent if farmers were banned from planting genetically modified beets. In 2010, a judge threw out the USDA's initial approval for the use of genetically modified seeds, saying, "it hadn't done enough research into the environmental impact" (Tomson, 2010, para. 2). Berezow (2012) noted that GE food research had produced a line of reduced allergen dairy milk, bananas in Africa that are resistant to a devastating bacterium that damages the livelihood of millions of people, healthier papayas in Hawaii (now saved from a ringspot virus), and an overall decreased use of insecticides because of increased crop resistance.

LAYPERSON NARRATIVES SUPPORTING PROP 37

Labeling advocates relied on redefining safety standards for consumers. First, this was enacted by pushing a "right to know" belief about GE food; and secondly, with reframing expectations surrounding current biotechnology science. Expectations surrounding food and drug information evolved as the FDA shaped early regulations concerning the safety and authenticity of U.S. food. With the evolution of food regulation, consumers expect to know the general composition of products (e.g., ingredients and nutritional value)

Other product details have been more recently contested. For example, labeling calories in restaurants and providing Country of Origin Labeling (COOL) were two additional novel debates appearing in the labeling industry. In this sense, perceptions of "right to know" issues have not solidified. Prop 37 advocates view genetic engineering as a characteristic worthy of sharing; hence, adding to preexisting labeling expectations. The right to know campaign, then, attempted to extend currently accepted consumer expectations.

The "right to know" about GE properties was a staple of campaign communication from the beginning of pro-Prop 37 messaging. As evidenced in the organization's namesake and first press release, pro-labeling advocates asserted that Californians had "'a right to know what's in the food [they] eat and feed [their] children'" (quote from Robyn O'Brien, author and founder of the Allergy Kids Foundation) (Fulbright, 2012). Also heavily emphasized was the assumption that those opposed to labeling were trying to hide information from consumers. For example, California's Right to Know television advertisement warned:

We've heard the false corporate health claims before. . . . Cigarettes aren't harmful. DDT is safe. Agent Orange is harmless. Now they say genetically engineered food is safe. If Monsanto and Dow think these foods are safe, why are they fighting our right to know what's in our food? (Malkan, 2012a)

Unabashedly, California Right to Know viewed labeling GE food as another fundamental right. The group's press releases acknowledged the need to know about GE food, something that Reeves also identified. Reeves further explained: "we want it [bioengineered food] out, it shouldn't be fed to kids, you know" (personal communication, 2013). Additionally, Reeves noted the importance of a book written by an author whose daughter experienced an anaphylactic allergic response to an Eggo waffle and Yoplait yogurt. Both foods "are chalked [*sic*] full of GMOs," so the problem is that "without any testing . . . there's really no evidence that they're safe, and without labeling there's no accountability" (Reeves, personal communication, 2013). Thus, California Right to Know insisted parents needed labels to avoid GE products in order to protect their families. Secondly, the Prop 37 supporters reframed and reinterpreted the scientific justification for labeling GE food.

Currently, the FDA allows GE food because known evidence documenting detrimental outcomes remains absent. This absence of negative outcomes could signal safety, but to Prop 37 advocates, absence was interpreted to mean: more testing is needed. Malkan (2012a) stated that the AMA and the World Health Organization/United Nations, "have said mandatory safety studies should be required," and to date the United States has failed to meet such standards. What's more is that the U.S. federal government "requires no safety studies for genetically engineered foods," and no long-term human trials with GE food have been implemented (Malkan, 2012a). Reeves echoed this sentiment noting, "there really has not been any testing" and "no evidence" that GE foods are safe (personal communication, 2013).

Closer to the election, a California Right to Know press release argued that blatant misrepresentations of "the positions of leading science, professional, academic organizations and government agencies" had plagued their campaign to deliver accurate information to consumers (Malkan, 2012e). Further, the only group that concluded biotech foods were safe was the American Council on Science and Health, "which happens to be a notorious front group for the pesticide and climate change deniers" (Malkan, 2012e).

Studies that supported alarming findings about GE food were also shared in press releases. On September 19, 2012, California Right to Know's press release entitled, "BREAKING: Massive Tumors in Rats Fed GMO Corn in First Ever Long-Term Study" reported that findings published in the *Journal of Food and Chemical Toxicology* indicated that GE corn yielded mammary tumors, kidney and liver damage, and other serious illnesses in rats (Malkan, 2012b). On September 25, 2012, Malkan (2012c) wrote that Russia suspended the import and use of Monsanto's GE corn, and the French government called for an investigation into GMOs. The same release noted, "the U.S. Food and Drug Administration has not reacted to the study" (Malkan, 2012c).

Prop 37 supporters reframed information about the science behind GE food. Pro-Prop 37 press releases specified that credible health and professional agencies generally acknowledged uncertainty surrounding GE food. Releases also suggested that emerging science found GE food was harmful to animals.

DISCUSSION AND IMPLICATIONS

In examining statements from the FDA and the pro-labeling California Right to Know, ascertaining which narrative has accurately construed the available evidence is difficult. Following, U.S. consumers were left unsure of whether or not they should worry about GE food. Consumers may also have been unsure whether or not the FDA was effectively regulating food and if multi-national companies were insensitive to the public's well-being. This section offers conclusions and implications regarding Prop 37 debate and its conflicting narratives.

California residents who joined California's Right to Know coalition committed themselves in support of labeling GE food. Further, many of these consumers believed that GE food was not only different from naturally produced food, but also that it was potentially harmful. These consumers construed or "infer[ed] meaning by assessing the importance and accuracy of the information and the authenticity of the source" to reach a conclusion that GE products posed significant risks (Sellnow et al., 2009, p. 8).

Many in the scientific community believed that, in reaching this conclusion, mis-construal had occurred. As McGloughlin noted, several California counties (like Marin and Mendocino) passed GE labeling laws locally (personal communication, 2013). Some bills, however, like Mendocino's, were "so poorly written," they "describe DNA as a complex protein" (when it's actually a nucleic acid) (McGloughlin, personal communication, 2013). Past local bills "also refer to mixing of species." However, "all of Mendocino, and in fact, all of production vineyards involve grafting one variety of grape onto another" (McGloughlin, personal communication, 2013). Should local laws be passed and actually enforced, those who propelled the bill forward would "already not [be] in compliance with their own law" (McGloughlin, personal communication, 2013). Unfortunately, it seems that the endearing, homegrown grass roots advocacy in this instance led Prop 37 voters astray.

Twenty years after the FDA released its initial statement of policy on new plant varieties, the agency has yet to find any human health consequences with GE food. Foods from GE plants "must meet the same requirements, including safety requirements, as foods from traditionally bred plants" (FDA, 2013a). Nutritional assessments for GE food "that have been evaluated by FDA through the consultation process have shown that foods are generally as nutritious as foods from comparable traditionally bred plants" (FDA, 2013a). Additionally, GE foods evaluated by the FDA "have not been more likely to

cause an allergic or toxic reaction than foods from traditionally bred plants"
(FDA, 2013a). All of FDA's testing (performed by scientists with back-
grounds in "genetic engineering, toxicology, chemistry, nutrition") indicated
no significant differences between GE food and traditionally-bred varieties
(FDA, 2013a). In this instance, the FDA remained neutral, unemotional, and
uninvolved in the debate over GE foods.

STRATEGIES FOR END USERS

The emerging gap between existing science and consumer perceptions is
growing. As additional states follow in Vermont's footsteps, mis-construal
should be addressed. Considering, FDA seems to have *lost control of its narrative* by failing to provide a spokesperson and a strategic direction for the
voice of science. But what could FDA have done differently?

Use Plain Language and Similarity

Groups like California Right to Know claimed that GE food should be
regarded and responded to in a manner congruent with that of cigarettes,
DDT, and Agent Orange (Malkan, 2012a). However, claims associating GE
food with the risk levels evidenced by these products are incorrect. While
cigarettes, for example, show clear association with several types of cancer,
the FDA has not established associations between GE food consumption and
negative human health outcomes.

In beginning to alleviate misconstrued information, consumers must
recognize misappropriated risk. This task is not impossible. For example,
misconstrued risks were once associated with microwaves. James Murray,
a professor of animal sciences at the University of California at Davis, says
that fears surrounding GE foods sound similar to "concerns about microwave
ovens, which some people initially thought would give off dangerous radia-
tion" (Ritter & Borenstein, 2010, para. 35). Learning the technical outcomes
of consuming GE foods is imperative; yet instead of learning new information about technology (as is the case with the introduction of a microwave),
learning entails diving into the compositional similarity of GE and naturally
bred food. Thus, promoting understanding entails using plain language and
highlighting the similarity of GE and non-GE products.

Develop a Plan and Elect a Spokesperson

Secondly, the FDA suffered from a lack of recognition of current regulations.
For example, in a California Right to Know press release, a spokesperson

is quoted as saying, "it is a scandal that the FDA, EPA, and companies like Monsanto have failed to do long-term testing over the past decade. Until further research is done we should have a moratorium on new approval of GE crops and labeling" (Malkan, 2012d). According to the FDA, "foods, such as fruits, vegetables, grains, and their byproducts, derived from plant varieties developed by the new methods of genetic modification are regulated within the existing framework of the act . . . that [applies] to foods developed by traditional plant breeding" (FDA, 1992). Arguably, GE food is even safer than traditionally bred varieties. McGloughlin stated that "genetic engineering is more precise and predictable" than traditionally bred products, yet it is "regulated up the wazoo" (Ritter & Borenstein, 2010, para. 20). Not only is GE food more carefully constructed compositionally than traditionally bred varieties, allowing scientists to remove unwanted traits, it is more heavily scrutinized. Considering the illegitimacy of the FDA with Prop 37 supporters, the FDA should also consider *creating a communication plan and electing a spokesperson* to direct its narrative and minimize further mis-construal.

California Right to Know successfully launched a cohesive messaging campaign, and narrowly missed success in enacting new labeling laws in the state. Prop 37's 47.1 percent favorability in the November 2012, election indicated significant support for both sides of the issue (California Secretary of State, 2012). California Right to Know quickly adapted and increased both its media presence and a diverse network of coalitions. The group also reframed information about the science behind GE food, and communicated messages of uncertainty surrounding the validity of testing of products. Lastly, a strong push to create identification with grassroots organizations and democratic values further helped bolster legitimacy for the movement. The FDA simply could not keep up.

Labeling GE food is gaining legitimacy, as exemplified by its narrow margin of failure in California and other concurrent deliberations in the United States. As activist groups increase momentum to support future efforts for GE food labeling and restriction, communication efforts that combat risk mis-construal are necessary for consumers to make an informed choice about the foods they buy and consume.

Agencies, such as the FDA, are limited in their capacity to participate in public debates about the safety of GE foods. Organizational policy and precedent limit the FDA's range of communication options. The agency is also unable to serve as an advocate on issues like genetic engineering because of the need to remain an objective regulatory agency. It is, however, completely within their capacity to rationalize and illuminate decisions surrounding new biotechnology and the implications for products. Understanding these decisions increases organizational transparency and shows consumers that the agency is engaging in ongoing monitoring, cataloging, regulation, and testing of genetic engineering and other innovations.

Additionally, groups outside the FDA who advocate for GE food, including outside of the labeling issue, may soon be compelled to increase public discussion surrounding the benefits associated with GE food. However, for obvious reasons, leaving for-profit organizations (i.e., Monsanto) to control the pro-GE food narrative is not a promising means to bolster the confidence of undecided parties. Biotechnology will be even more important in the next ten to twenty years as climate change and a growing global population puts more strain on current agricultural practices and yields. Without biotechnology, current agricultural outputs will struggle to feed four billion people, let alone the current seven billion or projected nine billion in coming years (McGloughlin, personal communication, 2013). More communication by those who see advantages to biotechnology is needed to reframe misconstrued evidence.

CONCLUSION

Twenty years after the FDA developed policy concerning GE foods, a resurgence of debate and criticism arose over the issue in California. Supporters of Proposition 37 launched a campaign in the state to pass legislation by popular vote in the November 2012 election. Policy advocates asserted that opponents to the bill claimed: "a) there's no proof that G.M.O.'s are harmful to humans, and b) studies demonstrating that they might be are largely flawed. Point B might even be true, although since the chemical companies largely control the research, it's hard to tell" (Bittman, 2012, para. 2). Opponents to labeling found that many supporters "don't actually have a genuine issue . . . but when you drill down you realize what their real issue is, their real issue is Monsanto" (McGloughlin, personal communication, 2013). Unfortunately, these tensions between local, organic, or natural coalitions and multi-national corporations have misconstrued the actual risk levels associated with GE food. This arbitrary calculation stands to provoke unnecessary and costly changes in the food system should other states continue pursuing similar labeling measures. As groups like California Right to Know continue to campaign and direct public dialogue, scientists, regulators, and companies will have a difficult time presenting counter narratives unless they refine their communication efforts by (1) explaining the true (i.e., technical risk) of GE foods and finally (2) reestablishing the legitimacy of the FDA with the public.

REFERENCES

Beecher, C. (2013, March 15). Whole Foods to require labeling of GMO foods. *Food Safety News*. Retrieved from http://www.foodsafetynews.com/2013/03/whole-foods-to-require-labeling-of-gmo-foods/

Berezow, A. (2012, October 17). Biotechnology on the ballot. *Wall Street Journal.* Retrieved from http://online.wsj.com/news/articles/SB10000872396390444486820 4578062832008000260

Bittman, M. (2012, October 23). Buying the vote on G.M.O.'s. *New York Times.* Retrieved from http://opinionator.blogs.nytimes.com/2012/10/23/buying-the-vote-on-g-m-o-s/?ref=opinion

Bowen, D. (2012). California general election voter guide. Retrieved from http://vig .cdn.sos.ca.gov/2012/general/pdf/complete-vig-v2.pdf

California Secretary of State. (2012). Statement of vote. Retrieved from http://www .sos.ca.gov/elections/sov/2012–general/sov-complete.pdf

Dowling, J., & Pfeffer, J. (1975). Organizational legitimacy: Social values and organizational behavior. *Pacific Sociological Review, 18*(1), 122–136. Retrieved from http://www.jstor.org/stable/1388226

Food and Drug Administration (FDA). (1992). Statement of policy—Food derived from new plant varieties. Retrieved from http://www.fda.gov/Food/Guid anceRegulation/GuidanceDocumentsRegulatoryInformation/Biotechnology/ucm 096095.htm

FDA. (2001). Guidance for industry: Voluntary labeling indicating whether foods have or have not been developed using bioengineering; Draft guidance. Retrieved from http://www.fda.gov/Food/GuidanceRegulation/GuidanceDocumentsRegula toryInformation/LabelingNutrition/ucm059098.htm

FDA. (2013a). Questions & answers on food from genetically engineered plants. Retrieved from http://www.fda.gov/Food/FoodScienceResearch/Biotechnology/ ucm346030.htm

FDA. (2013b). FDA's role in regulating safety of GE foods. Retrieved from http:// www.fda.gov/ForConsumers/ConsumerUpdates/ucm352067.htm

Flynn, D. (2015, June 24). State legislatures pass on adopting gmo-labeling policies this year. *Food Safety News.* Retrieved from http://www.foodsafetynews.com/ 2015/06/states-pass-on-opportunities-to-jump-ahead-of-feds-on-gmo-labeling-pol icy/#.VZ3bkGA4SfS

Fulbright, L. (2012, April 30). *California ballot initiative to require labeling of genetically engineered foods submitted to Attorney General* [Press release]. Retrieved from http://www.carighttoknow.org/california_ballot_initiative_submitted

Heath, R. L. (2004). Telling a story: A narrative approach to communication during crisis. In D. P. Millar & R. L. Heath (Eds.) *Responding to crisis: A rhetorical approach to crisis communication* (pp. 167–188). Mahwah, NJ: Lawrence Erlbaum Associates.

Jargon, J., & Berry, I. (2012, October 25). Dough rolls out to fight "engineered" label on food. *Wall Street Journal.* Retrieved from http://online.wsj.com/article/SB1000 14240529702034006045780731829071237601.html

Leschin-Hoar, C. (2013, March 13). Prop. 37 died, but the food-labeling fight lives. *Voice of San Diego.* Retrieved from http://voiceofsandiego.org/2013/03/13/prop-37–died-but-the-food-labeling-fight-lives/

Littlefield, R. S. (2015). Improving how we communicate about infectious disease risks. *Microbe, 10,* 1–4.

Littlefield, R. S., Farell, L., Beauchamp, K., & Rathnasinghe, S. (2012). Maintaining relationships with the public: Applications of relational dialectics theory in crisis communication. Paper presented at the National Communication Association Convention, Orlando, Florida.

Malkan, S. (2012a, August 27). *Prop 37's first TV ad: No on 37 run by same companies that told us DDT and Agent Orange was safe* [Press release]. Retrieved from http://www.carighttoknow.org/first_television_ads

Malkan, S. (2012b, September 19). *Breaking: Massive tumors in rats fed GMO corn in first ever long-term study* [Press release]. Retrieved from http://www.carightto know.org/new_study

Malkan, S. (2012c, September 25). *Russia suspends imports of genetically engineered corn in wake of rat study; France orders probe of GMOs* [Press release]. Retrieved from http://www.carighttoknow.org/russia_suspends_imports_of_monsanto_corn

Malkan, S. (2012d, October 13). *Health leaders renew calls for Prop 37 in wake of science controversy* [Press release]. Retrieved from http://www.carighttoknow.org/ health_leaders

Malkan, S. (2012e, November 2). *Documented deceptions of No on 37 campaign* [Press release]. Retrieved from http://www.carighttoknow.org/documented_deceptions

Palenchar, M. J., & Heath, R. L. (2002). Another part of the risk communication model: Analysis of communication processes and message content. *Journal of Public Relations Research, 14*(2), 127–158. doi: 10.1207/S1532754XJPRR1402_3

Petrun, E. L., Flood, A., Sellnow, T. L., Smith Edge, M., & Burns, K. (2015). Shaping health perceptions: Effectively communicating about chemicals in food. *Food Protection Trends, 35*(1), 24–45.

Pollan, M. (2012, October 10). Vote for the dinner party. *New York Times*. Retrieved from http://www.nytimes.com/2012/10/14/magazine/why-californias-proposi tion-37–should-matter-to-anyone-who-cares-about-food.html?pagewanted=all&_r=0

Ritter, M., & Borenstein, S. (2010, October 3). Scientists weighing altered salmon. *The Washington Post*. Retrieved from http://www.washingtonpost.com/wp-dyn/ content/article/2010/10/02/AR2010100200340.html

Rottenstreich, Y., & Hsee, C. K. (2001). Money, kisses, and electric shocks: On the affective psychology of risk. *Psychological Science, 12*(3), 185–190. doi: 10. 1111/1467–9280.00334

Scherer, C. W., & Juanillo, N. K. (2003). The continuing challenge of community health risk management and communication. In T. L. Thompson, A. Dorsey, K. Miller, & R. Parrott (Eds.), *Handbook of health communication* (pp. 221–239). Mahwah, NJ: Lawrence Erlbaum Associates.

Sellnow, T. L., Ulmer, R. R., Seeger, M. W., Littlefield, R. S. (2009). *Effective risk communication: A message centered approach*. New York: Springer Science + Business Media, LLC.

Sinaceur, M., Heath, C., & Cole, S. (2005). Emotional and deliberative reactions to a public crisis: Mad cow disease in France. *Psychological Science, 16*(3), 247–254. Retrieved from http://www.jstor.org/stable/40064209

Slovic, P., Finucane, M., Peters, E., & MacGregor, D. G. (2002). The affect heuristic. In T. Gilovich, D. Griffin, & D. Kahneman (Eds.), *Heuristics and biases: The psychology of intuitive judgment* (pp. 397–420). Cambridge: Cambridge University Press.

Slovic, P., Finucane, M. L., Peters, E., & MacGregor, D. G. (2004). Risk analysis and risk as feelings: Some thoughts about affect, reason, risk, and rationality. *Risk Analysis, 24*(2), 311–322. doi: 10.1111/j.0272–4332.2004.00433.x

Specter, M. (2012, November 2). The seed wars. *New Yorker.* Retrieved from http://www.newyorker.com/online/blogs/comment/2012/11/voting-on-genetically-engineered-food-in-california.html

Spiegelman, A. (2012, February 17). The spark behind the California right to know genetically engineered food act of 2012. *Huffington Post.* Retrieved from http://www.huffingtonpost.com/annie-spiegelman/genetically-engineered-food_b_1245023.html

Tomson, B. (2010, October 18). Ruling imperils sugar production. *Wall Street Journal.* Retrieved from http://online.wsj.com/article/SB10001424052702304250404575558071139328364.html

U.S. Department of Agriculture (USDA). (2013). Biotechnology frequently asked questions (FAQs). Retrieved from http://usda.gov/wps/portal/usda/usdahome?contentid=BiotechnologyFAQs.xml&navid=AGRICULTURE

Walsh, B. (2012, November 6). Prop 37: Why California's ballot initiative on GM food is about politics more than science. *Time.* Retrieved from http://science.time.com/2012/11/06/prop-37–why-californias-ballot-initiative-on-gm-food-is-about-politics-more-than-science/

Wilce, R. (2013, March 15). GMO labeling passes Vermont house as activists prepare to march against Monsanto. *PR Watch.* Retrieved from http://www.prwatch.org/news/2013/05/12108/gmo-labeling-passes-vermont-house-activists-prepare-march-against-monsanto

Yin, R. K. (2003). *Case study research: Designs and method* (3rd ed.). Thousand Oaks, CA: Sage.

Chapter Eight

The Tension of Emotional Connection

Health Literacy and the 2010 Salmonella *Egg Recall*

Holly A. Roberts and Shari R. Veil

Health literacy is defined as "[the] degree to which individuals have the capacity to obtain, process, and understand basic health information and services needed to make appropriate health decisions" (Kutner, Greenberg, Jin, & Paulsen, 2006, p. iii). Much of the research on health literacy has focused on the doctor-patient relationship and how to improve the explanation of medical terms and choices in clinical visits. However, individuals face health decisions everyday, and not all situations allow for thorough explanations of the health risks at hand. Particularly in crises that create health risks, like foodborne outbreaks, individuals with limited health literacy are at even more of a disadvantage. Notices of recalls are often broadcasted on the evening news; but rarely provide instructional information on how to protect oneself from the associated health risks. Those with limited health literacy may, therefore, not have enough background knowledge or understand how to access additional information regarding effective self-protective actions.

During such a crisis, responsible organizations must work to create, maintain, and balance an emotional connection with the affected publics. This connection encompasses many elements including the manner by which the messages are distributed and the content they include. In order to display sensitivity, messages should accurately target those who need information to remain safe (Sellnow, Ulmer, Seeger, & Littlefield, 2009). Such information needs to be presented in a language and format that increases understanding. Thus, in a health crisis, communicating agencies and organizations must account for the health literacy of the affected stakeholders to effectively establish an emotional connection.

In April 2010, authorities noted a rise in reported cases of *Salmonella* serotype *Enteritidis* and ultimately identified Wright County Egg/Hillsdale Farms, both based in Iowa, as the sources of the contamination. The Centers for Disease

Control and Prevention (CDC) and the Food and Drug Administration (FDA) disseminated press releases and held joint press conferences warning the public of the contaminated eggs and providing instructional messages on how individuals should protect themselves from the foodborne outbreak. While the media did cover the outbreak, the instructional messages regarding how to make effective risk decisions were typically not included in the broadcast news stories. As waves of recalls persisted throughout the summer of 2010, the media coverage changed from an alert to the recall to an investigation of the many atrocities in food safety; in other words, from forms of bacteria to bureaucratic processes. The fact that people were still getting violently ill was no longer news, and without sufficient warnings and instructional messages outlining how to prevent the spread of the outbreak, audiences, and particularly those individuals with limited health literacy, were left without the knowledge or wherewithal to make appropriate health decisions.

This chapter examines the health communication strategies employed by officials, responsible organizations, and the media providing the public with accurate, understandable information in a timely manner during a foodborne outbreak. Specifically, we discuss the importance of health literacy considerations and compassion when communicating food safety concerns, and critically examine the development and delivery of messages during the 2010 egg recall. First, we describe the constraints of health literacy and discuss the theoretical underpinnings of the dialectical tension of emotional connection. We then outline the case and analyze the media coverage of the egg recall. Finally, we assess the ability of officials and the media to address the dialectical tension of emotional connection and offer strategies for end users to improve communication in foodborne outbreaks.

CULTURAL CONTEXT

Health literacy requires an individual to possess at least the basic skills of being able to read as well as listen and to possess the ability to make decisions while being analytical. In addition to these skills, an individual must be, "visually literate (able to understand graphs or other visual information), computer literate (able to operate a computer), information literate (able to obtain and apply relevant information), and numerically or computationally literate (able to calculate or reason numerically)," and be able to apply all these skills to the area of health (National Network of Libraries of Medicine, 2010, para. 2 & 5). Adequate health literacy implies that the individual has the ability to understand appointment reminders, medical brochures, consent forms, a doctor's directions, and the printed instructions on prescription bottles. Individuals also must be able to negotiate through complex health care systems (National Network of Libraries of Medicine, 2010).

The health literacy of a population creates a unique cultural constraint that may hinder the ability of organizations to adequately communicate with their intended audience(s). To establish effective crisis communication, a company must work to not only identify the health literacy level of its stakeholders, but decision-makers must also create and distribute messages in a culturally sensitive and appropriate manner. Additionally, this cultural consideration identifies new vulnerable populations. While a specific health risk may be greater for selected individuals—in this case, *Salmonella* is particularly problematic for infants and the elderly (CDC, 2010c)—the health literacy level of an individual who normally may not have been considered as a member of a vulnerable population may now place himself/herself at greater risk due to an inability to understand health messages.

To assess the health literacy of the American population, the National Assessment of Adult Literacy conducted a survey and divided participants into four main categories: proficient, intermediate, basic, or below basic (Kutner et al., 2006). Those with proficient literacy comprised 12 percent of the participants, and just over half (53 percent) were found to have intermediate health literacy skills; while 22 percent possessed basic health literacy skills, and 14 percent possessed below basic health literacy skills. According to the survey, thirty million people aged sixteen and above are unable to understand anything above the most simple and concrete messages. Demographics did play a role in the likelihood of an individual to fall into a specific category. For example, adults aged sixty-five and older had lower average health literacy skills than adults aged twenty-five to thirty-nine. Blacks, Hispanics, American Indian/Alaskan Native, and other multicultural adults had lower average health literacy skills than Whites and Asian/Pacific Islanders (Kutner et al., 2006).

Where individuals received their heath information was also a factor. Results indicated that as health literacy decreased, so did the percentage of adults who got information about health issues from family members, coworkers, or friends. Individuals with proficient, intermediate, and basic skill levels were more likely to obtain health information from written sources (newspapers, magazines, books, and Internet) than were adults with below basic skills (Kutner et al., 2006). Also, a higher percentage of adults with basic or below basic health literacy skills received information regarding health issues from radio and television.

Health campaigns have traditionally relied heavily on the media to communicate their message(s). While six in ten Americans, approximately 59 percent get their news from a blend of offline and online news sources (Pew

Research Center, 2010); television, specifically, is the most commonly used media in crisis situations due to its delivery of immediate information with visual aids (Heath & O'Hair, 2010). For crises that increased health risks, Lewis and Lewis (2008) encouraged officials to provide still photos or videos to the media for inclusion in television and Internet coverage in order to meet the needs of audience members from all health literacy levels. Average Americans get frustrated with the slow transmission of information, read only from left to right, and are attracted to bright colors and images; these are additional constraints to consider when trying to reach audiences with important health information (Glik, 2007).

In a crisis, spokespersons and responsible organizations must balance the need to provide information while addressing the feelings of those at risk. The following discussion of the dialectical tension of emotional connection recognizes the importance of communicating health information with compassion.

DIALECTICAL TENSION OF EMOTIONAL CONNECTION

When addressing the dialectical tension of emotional connection, organizations should be aware that messages may be viewed along a spectrum of sensitive to insensitive. Crisis communication best practices, outlined by Seeger (2006), suggested communicating with concern and empathy when addressing stakeholders. These messages of sensitivity "enhance the credibility of the message and enhance the perceived legitimacy of the messenger both before and after an event" (Seeger, 2006, p. 241). Furthermore, Seeger claimed that the public was more likely to respond positively to spokespersons who acknowledged any harm that may have occurred if they expressed that concern with compassion. Sellnow, Wickline, and Veil (2013) furthered this perspective by recognizing that even when the organization is not responsible for the crisis (e.g., such as a natural disaster), spokespersons should still acknowledge the pain and suffering of affected stakeholders. These actions become crucial to crisis communication; in that, "if the public sees an expression of genuine concern and empathy, it has more faith that the actions being undertaken or recommended are appropriate and legitimate" (Seeger, 2006, p. 241).

In addition to the best practice of communicating with compassion, Sellnow and Vidoloff (2009) suggested the best practice of acknowledging and accounting for cultural differences. They argued: "standard communication forms, including the media, are unlikely to reach underrepresented populations"; and crisis communicators must dedicate additional time and resources to reaching these populations (p. 42). Littlefield, Farrell, Beauchamp, and Rathnasinghe (2012) also addressed this concern about crisis communication in their description of the dialectical tension of emotional connection. They indicated that this tension stemmed from "the best practices of hearing and understanding public concerns, as well as being open, candid, and honest with the public" (p. 13).

Crisis communication scholars also suggest that messages should be tailored to "meet the needs, interests and expectations" of the audience (Sellnow & Mountford, 2011, p. 331), based not only on demographic information, geographic uniqueness, and language, but also on the basis of emotional need. While fear is a predominant emotion during crisis, Veil and Husted (2012) recognized a myriad of other emotions affecting an organization and stakeholders; including anger, sadness, and confusion. They concluded "recognizing emotions and communicating compassionately will minimize emotional harm to victims and reputational harm to the organization" (p. 134).

In the Salmonella egg recall, the responsible organizations and media not only should have been aware of the health literacy of the affected population, but their messages should have been sensitive to and constructed in a manner that would have appealed to the audience. Those responding, and particularly those responsible, also should have included apologia for the pain and suffering of the stakeholders in the crisis messages (Sellnow, Wickline, & Veil, 2013). Insensitivity results from the failure to create and distribute information according to the practices outlined above; thereby affecting the image of the responsible organizations and the effectiveness of their messages.

RESEARCH QUESTIONS

To better understand health literacy and the dialectical tension of emotional connection in the 2010 egg recall, this study sought to answer the two research questions:

RQ1: How did the responsible organizations and media navigate the dialectical tension of emotional connection during the *Salmonella* egg recall of 2010?

RQ2: How did the cultural context of health literacy affect the ability of the responsible organizations and media to resolve the crisis?

CRISIS TIMELINE

Salmonella is a type of bacteria that can cause infection with fever, diarrhea, and abdominal cramps. The illness usually ranges in length from four to seven days, and while antibiotics can help treat an individual, sometimes hospitalization is required. In some severe cases, death can occur. Infants, the elderly, and those with weak immune systems are typically more prone to severe cases of the disease. While most people recover fully from the disease, a small number of people have long-term effects, including eye irritation, painful urination, and joint pain. These effects can last for months or even years and can lead to chronic arthritis, which is difficult to treat (CDC, 2010c). The CDC estimates that approximately 1,939 people were sickened with *Salmonella* serotype *Enteritidis* infections during the crisis (CDC, 2010c).

The following timeline, separated by the three stages of crisis, briefly outlines the health crisis surrounding the Salmonella egg recall of 2010. Particular focus is given to communication strategies used by agencies and organizations as a background for the media analysis.

Table 8.1. Crisis Timeline for 2010 Egg Recall

Pre-Crisis	
Date	*Event*
1994–2010	Jack Decoster (Wright County Egg owner) is charged with animal cruelty, environmental violations, sexual harassment, and employment of illegal immigrants.
April 2010	The first reports of *Salmonella Enteritidis* were identified.

Crisis	
Date	*Event*
August 13, 2010	Wright County Egg issued a recall of eggs from three of its farms.
August 16, 2010	The CDC posted information to its website.
August 18, 2010	Wright County Egg issued a recall of eggs from all five of its farms. This recall included eggs shipped on or after May 16, 2010, approximately 380 million eggs sold under twenty-three different brand names.
August 20, 2010	Hillsdale Farms issued a recall of approximately 170 million eggs sold under five different brand names.
August 20, 2010	The FDA posted a press release on its website.
August 23, 2010	Hillsdale Farms furthered its recall to include 24,300 additional eggs sold under four different brand names (including Hillandale).

Post-Crisis	
Date	*Event*
October 18, 2010	The FDA authorized Hillandale Farms to resume egg shipments.
October 18, 2010	The FDA issued a warning letter to Quality Egg LLC to correct unsanitary conditions.
November 30, 2010	The FDA approved the first shipment of eggs to leave Quality Egg.

(FDA, 2010b, 2010c, 2010d; Iannelli, 2010; Jalonick, 2010)

METHOD

To develop the context of the case, official press releases and statements posted to the websites of the organizations and agencies deemed accountable for the crisis response during the 2010 *Salmonella* egg recall were examined. We determined the accountable organizations to be the U.S. Food and Drug Administration (FDA) and Centers for Disease Control and Prevention (CDC) as well as the implicated egg suppliers, Wright County Egg/Hillsdale Farms. The press releases and statements were analyzed to determine what messages for self-protection were provided to the media by the agencies and organizations. Additionally, the delivery and content of the statements were analyzed for elements of sensitivity or insensitivity regarding an understanding of the cultural constraints of those affected by the recall.

In addition to the official statements posted, we conducted a content analysis of the televised coverage of the crisis from August 13–20, 2010. The researchers used the television tracking system housed in a southeastern university to search for the keywords, "salmonella" and "eggs." If either of these words, or combinations of these words, were found in a television segment, the segment was isolated and captured for further analysis. A total of 566 videos were captured during the search. Stations included in analysis were CNN, CNNH, CSPAN, CW, CBS, Fox, FNC, NBC, ABC, PBS, and MSNBC. Broadcasts were coded for presence or absence of instructional messages, image restoration tactics, and messages of self-protection, among other items. Two coders observed and coded 20 percent of the videos to establish reliability before coding the remaining data. Intercoder reliability was calculated using Scott's *Pi* (1955). Reliability was found to be acceptable for each theme with the minimum agreement at or above 90.1 percent ($p = 0.84$). The content and delivery of the mediated messages were also critically analyzed for elements of sensitivity or insensitivity, regarding an understanding the cultural constraints of those affected by the recall.

Table 8.2. Coding Criteria and Coding Examples

Continuum Anchor	Dialectical Tension	Continuum Anchor	Coding Criteria and Coding Examples
Sensitive	Emotional Connection ◆———◆	Insensitive	◆ Sensitive: Messages reflect an empathetic emotional connection. (For example: *"We are deeply sorry . . ."*) ◆ Insensitive: Messages do not reflect an emotional connection. (For example: *"Contact our lawyers for information . . ."*)

ANALYSIS

The crisis for the public began with the first cases of *Salmonella*; however, it was not until the media were alerted to the recall that the contamination became a true crisis for the offending organizations.

Pre-Crisis

While the first cases of *Salmonella* were reported as early as April 2010, the link to Wright County Eggs was not confirmed and the first recall was not issued until August 13, 2010. The CDC posted the first press release with instructional messages for self-protection three days later. The FDA did not post instructional messages until Hillendale Eggs was identified on August 20, 2010, as another source of the contamination.

Crisis

The CDC posted information on its website providing the public with tips to reduce their risk of contracting *Salmonella* from eggs. The website stated that like other foods, eggs can be safe if handled properly. The website listed the following items as specific actions an individual could take to reduce the risk of contracting the disease:

1. Keep eggs refrigerated at ≤ 45° F (≤7° C) at all times.
2. Discard cracked or dirty eggs.
3. Wash hands and all food contact surface areas (counter tops, utensils, and cutting boards) with soap and water after contact with raw eggs. Then disinfect the food contact surfaces using a sanitizing agent, such as bleach, following label instructions.
4. Eggs should be cooked until both the white and the yolk are firm and eaten promptly after cooking.
5. Do not keep eggs warm or at room temperature for more than two hours.
6. Refrigerate unused or leftover egg-containing foods promptly.
7. Avoid eating raw eggs.
8. Avoid restaurant dishes made with raw or undercooked, unpasteurized eggs. Restaurants should use pasteurized eggs in any recipe (such as Hollandaise sauce or Caesar salad dressing) that calls for raw eggs.
9. Consumption of raw or undercooked eggs should be avoided, especially by young children, elderly persons, and persons with weakened immune systems or debilitating illness. (CDC, 2010a)

The CDC also included similar information for egg producers and food service establishments (CDC, 2010b).

The first official press release from the FDA (2010a) was posted on August 20. Listed near the top of the site were the following "fast facts":

- The current recall of eggs in their shells, or "shell eggs," is part of an ongoing and intensive investigation by local, state, and federal officials into the cause of recent cases of *Salmonella* serotype *Enteritidis.*
- This recall affects shell eggs produced by Wright County Egg of Galt, Iowa. The eggs are packaged under different brand names and distributed nationwide.
- The shell eggs may contain *Salmonella* serotype *Enteritidis* (SE) and may cause serious illness.
- Salmonella can cause serious and sometimes fatal infections in young children, frail or elderly people, and others with weakened immune systems.
- Consumers should throw away the product or return the product to the store.

Listed further down the page, under the sixth heading was information explaining to the public the type of action they should take in order to keep themselves from contracting the disease. The information is listed as follows:

> Don't eat recalled eggs. Consumers who have recalled eggs should discard them or return them to their retailer for a refund. Individuals who think they might have become ill from eating recalled eggs should consult their health care providers. If consumers are unsure about the source of their eggs, they are urged not to eat them and to discard them immediately. (FDA, 2010a)

The press release also included the appropriate Julian date numbers that corresponded with the contaminated eggs (FDA, 2010a). However, the press release did not discuss what the numbers actually meant or where the consumer should look for them, thereby displaying a lack of cultural understanding in regards to health literacy.

Neither of the egg suppliers provided detailed instructions on how to handle recalled eggs; however, Hillsdale Farms (2010) did provide a description on its website of how to find out if a person had eggs subject to the recall:

> To identify if you have recalled eggs, look for the plant number code and Julian date stamped on the end of the egg carton or printed on the case label. The plant number begins with the letter P and then a four-digit number. The Julian date follows the plant number. For example: if your carton contains "P-1860 230" that means the plant number is P-1860, and the Julian date is 230. (para. 3)

This information not only mentioned the Julian numbers but also offered a brief explanation of what that meant and how the consumer should locate the information on the egg carton. This message by Hillsdale Farms did exhibit some understanding of the health literacy level of its audience. Hillandale Farms recognized that the average person may not know what a Julian date is and their message displays sensitivity to the needs of their stakeholders. Quality Egg LLC did not post any information regarding the recall on its site except for a letter to the residents of Maine stating that their eggs remain untainted (Quality Egg LLC, 2010).

While the CDC and the FDA did post messages to their websites, content analysis of the media coverage revealed that of the 566 videos coded, only 12 percent (n=69) of the broadcasts addressed the symptoms of *Salmonella*, 9 percent (n=50) mentioned specific demographics prone to falling ill with the disease, and 2 percent (n=12) provided instructional information for individuals who thought they may have *Salmonella* poisoning. Only 3 percent (n=19) instructed viewers to wash hands and cooking surfaces, 17 percent (n=95) instructed viewers to cook the eggs thoroughly, and 9 percent (n=49) provided information regarding plant numbers and Julian dates, key messages included in the CDC and FDA press releases. Instructional information was also lacking about the specific brand names of eggs that were infected with *Salmonella*. Only 3 percent (n=16) of the videos analyzed in the broadcast listed all the brands included in the recall. The most prominent message of instruction was where individuals could go to find more information on the recall. During the first week of the recall 32 percent (n=183) of the broadcasts provided a link to a website, typically the website of the news broadcaster, that then linked to the FDA and CDC websites. Television broadcast coverage did, of course, include visual elements. However, only 6 percent (n=33) included images with an instructional element (hand washing, Julian dates, disposal, etc.).

Three primarily frames were used in the media coverage of the egg recall. The first frame simply alerted the public to the recall. Stories focused on the number of eggs being recalled with images of eggs on conveyer belts. Many of the broadcasters made puns out of the recall, using headlines and taglines, such as: "Cracking the egg recall" and "FDA scrambles to solve the *Salmonella* outbreak." Conversations between broadcasters included comments about how they hoped their media counterparts had not eaten eggs for breakfast, and banter about how they did or did not enjoy runny yolks. The media coverage was not only insensitive to the health literacy of the audience, in that there was a scarcity of instructional information provided, but also the broadcasters' jokes and puns were clearly insensitive to viewers already suffering from foodborne illness.

The second frame of the coverage centered on how the FDA and the CDC collaborated on recalls and the pending legislation that would give FDA the power to better control food regulation. Interviews with FDA spokesperson,

Margaret Hamburg detailed why the FDA wasn't allowed to monitor egg safety. The FDA was a prominent source cited throughout the recall coverage analyzed, identified in 27 percent (n=154) of the broadcasts. The CDC was a source in 18 percent (n=101) of the broadcasts. However, despite the press releases including instructional messages for self-protection; in the media coverage, the FDA only provided instructional messages in 8 percent (n=44) of the messages and the CDC in less than 2 percent (n=11) of the messages. Neither Wright County Egg nor Hillandale Farms provided instructions for self-protection in their broadcast messages, thereby displaying overwhelming insensitivity.

Post-Crisis

The third media frame following the recall reported on Jack Decoster's tainted past. Accompanying images portrayed hen houses, animal rights activists, and unsatisfied employees. Elements of image restoration from the egg companies were identified in 9 percent (n=49) of the broadcasts. Of the strategies provided, 10 percent (n=6) were considered negative strategies, including blame shifting and defeasibility. The majority of the videos with image restoration strategies contained bolstering techniques (64 percent; n=36), with many of them assuring the public that the egg producers were working with the government agencies to correct the situation. Finally, 2 percent (n=1) of the videos displayed minimizing strategies, 21 percent (n=12) showed mortification, and 27 percent (n=15) contained elements of recompense/corrective action.

Some of the image restoration strategies were contradictory. For example, during a congressional hearing, Jack Decoster, owner of Quality Egg LLC (parent company of Wright County Egg) issued an apology, "We were horrified to learn that our eggs may have made people sick . . . we apologize to everyone who may have been sickened by eating our eggs'" (Harris, 2010, para. 3). And then, during the testimony of Peter Decoster, son of Jack Decoster and COO of Wright County Egg (one of the offending organizations), he claimed that the *Salmonella* most likely came from a separate company and that, "[the] filthy conditions documented by the FDA were standard practice in the industry" (Harris, 2010, para 6). Representatives from Hillsdale Farms declined to testify during the hearings but did send an e-mail to the congressional subcommittee stating that they were working to disassociate from Jack Decoster entirely (Harris, 2010).

CONCLUSION

Previous research has developed critical, beneficial information that should be capitalized upon for effective communication in a crisis. This information becomes even more important during a health related crisis, especially one that affects individuals with varied levels of health literacy. The most alarming finding in this case study was the lack of instructional information provided to keep the public safe. The dearth of instructional information identifying the specific demographic groups prone to falling ill, and actions that should be taken to protect themselves is disconcerting.

Yet, another area of concern was the lack of explanation surrounding Julian numbers. First, the FDA did mention Julian numbers, but the Hillandale Farms web site actually explained what Julian numbers were to the public. This explanation was beneficial because as members of a population struggle with health literacy, individuals may not posses that knowledge (Kutner at al., 2006). The lack of instructional information (hand washing, Julian numbers, and egg cooking) that actually appeared in the news coverage demonstrates a lack of compassion for individuals who, as health literacy research suggests, may not have the initial knowledge to understand that these actions are necessary to keep themselves safe in a health crisis.

Those with lower health literacy, such as the elderly, who according to the CDC (2010c) were more likely to suffer severe forms of *Salmonella*, may not have been properly targeted during this recall. For example, the Pew Research Center (2010) found individuals over the age of fifty comprised a significant portion of the individuals who obtained their news from the television and local print media. And yet, the FDA only posted its press releases online and, when FDA officials did host a briefing with the CDC, they were not aired on television, one of the primary sources for individuals with basic or below basic health literacy skills (Kutner et al., 2006). Inadequately distributing messages to affected audiences demonstrates a lack of emotional connection with stakeholders. Not only does it acknowledge a deficit in understanding those affected by the recall, but also an indifference to those who may not have had the ability and/or access to appropriate media channels.

Spokespersons also were a concern during the egg recall of 2010. As the media analysis revealed, a very small portion of information was cited as coming from a government agency or an egg producer, resulting in the anchor men/women serving as the key information providers. This was problematic in that, as Seeger (2006) explained, the public is more likely to respond positively to spokespersons who acknowledge harm and express concern. Because the media channels distributing the messages were responsible for neither the recall nor the damage it caused, they also were not responsible to apologize for the crisis. Therefore, the quality of the message and the effectiveness of its instructional content may have been hindered based upon the lack of apologia and concern with which it was being delivered.

Additionally, as Glik (2007) discussed, images are very helpful when communicating important information. In this particular case, images of the recall dates on the egg cartons or a demonstration on how to make sure the egg is cooked to 160 degrees would have been considered the best method in communicating during this crisis; especially since the press releases were posted online, and as the Pew Research Center (2010) pointed out, 66 percent of individuals go to the Internet for information pertaining to health and medicine. However, these types of images rarely appeared in the coverage. Instead, images of eggs, chickens, and farms were shown providing little to no help to a population who may have relied on images to help them understand the health crisis at hand. Once again, these actions demonstrated a poor understanding of the affected publics and a lack of sensitivity to their needs and concerns, As Sellnow and Vidoloff (2009) suggested, reaching the underrepresented populations—in this case those struggling with health literacy—should have been a focus of the organization and media involved.

Furthermore, while image restoration strategies were present, these also demonstrated a lack of sensitivity to those affected by the recall. With such a small percentage of videos indicating recompense and mortification, sensitive messages were largely missing from the coverage. The remaining strategies of bolstering and minimization can be construed as wholly insensitive to a population struggling with health literacy and at risk of contracting *Salmonella*.

Two issues of insensitivity arose during media coverage of the crisis. The first was the shift in coverage from the details of the recall and how individuals should remain safe from harm to the dramatic coverage of Jack Decoster's messy past and the pending FDA legislation. While related to the crisis at hand, these later frames did not provide helpful information to the population at risk. Additionally, the media's witty puns surrounding the coverage, such as using the words "scrambles" and "cracking," may have decreased their credibility by being insensitive to those afraid of contracting the disease. As mentioned by Seeger (2006), those who provide compassion and concern are more likely to appear credible to stakeholders. In essence, the media's attempts at humor amidst a health crisis hindered the ability of stakeholders to mitigate harm because anchormen/women were not seen as credible sources. Arguably, if the media were not taking the crisis seriously, why should the public? Additionally, because spokespersons should acknowledge the emotions of stakeholders during crisis to minimize harm to victims, failure to do so may be harmful to the organization(s) (Veil & Husted, 2012). Essentially, the media's disregard for the potential fear and confusion of the stakeholders appeared insensitive given the stakes at hand.

STRATEGIES FOR END USERS

There are four valuable lessons from this case study for organizations that may find themselves responsible for a health crisis, organizations that may be seen as experts during a crisis, and for media sources responsible for distributing important information related to a crisis.

Establish Partnerships

Establishing partnerships with the media and other organizations prior to a crisis is essential. Aside from being considered a best practice of crisis communication, this simple action can help eliminate problems that may arise from not knowing where to turn to gather information. For example, had partnerships been evident in this case, we may have seen more consistency in terms of reporting the cause and side effects of *Salmonella* from the FDA and CDC. Additionally, had a partnership been formed between the media and egg producers, information may have been accessible to the public earlier and it may have been more accurate because the media would have received information directly from the source, rather than attempting to find their own information. Furthermore, had a relationship been utilized during the crisis, more statements from the egg producers may have been conveyed, resulting in increased credibility for both the egg producers and the media, and other items, such as appropriate images, may have been readily available. Such strategies would have increased the emotional connection between the communicating entities and the stakeholders.

Utilize Appropriate Images

The use of images is also a learning point during this crisis. As Glik (2007) discussed, images are very helpful when communicating important information. In this particular case, images of the recall dates on the egg cartons or a demonstration on how to make sure the egg is cooked to 160 degrees would have been considered the best method in communicating during this crisis. The absence of these images reflected insensitivity on the part of the egg producers and the media because both entities were viewed as responsible for the gathering and distributing of necessary images explaining the actions necessary for stakeholders to keep themselves safe from harm.

Understand Risks and Stakeholders

It is important for responsible organizations and the media to fully understand the target audience. The egg producers, government agencies, and media did not always act appropriately in order to explain the health crisis to groups with varied rates of health literacy. Organizations should have a general understanding of their consumers' health literacy levels. Organizations should also know the potential risks and problems that could occur in their industry and be prepared to provide information to mitigate those hazards. Preemptive actions could lead to a better understanding of groups affected by the organization so that in the face of a crisis, the organization is more prepared to act quickly and appropriately to save its reputation and, ultimately, save lives.

Communicate with Sensitivity

A lasting implication from this study addresses the dialectical tension of emotional connection. As this research and the best practices suggest, organizations should always communicate with concern and compassion. Doing so increases the credibility of spokespersons and increases the likelihood that messages will be viewed positively and be followed. Furthermore, the media are not immune from this responsibility and should do their best to protect stakeholders, regardless of the actions of the responsible organizations. This responsibility includes maintaining credibility and following the suggestions listed above. Failure to do so results in an insensitive response, thereby damaging the reputation of the organizations and the media outlet. This could affect the credibility of the organization in the face of future crises; and ultimately, the success of the organization. In contrast, a sensitive response demonstrates effective audience analysis and genuine concern for the affected stakeholders. Such a response will bolster the reputation of the organization and media, therefore solidifying an emotional connection and favorable crisis outcome.

REFERENCES

CDC. (2010a, August 16). *Tips to reduce your risk of Salmonella from eggs*. Retrieved from http://www.cdc.gov/Features/SalmonellaEggs/

CDC. (2010b, September 27). *Salmonella*. Retrieved from http://www.cdc.gov/sal monella/general/

CDC. (2010c, October 19). *Investigation update: Multistate outbreak of human Salmonella Enteritidis infections associated with shell eggs*. Retrieved from http://www.cdc.gov/salmonella/enteritidis/

FDA. (2010a, August 20). *Urgent nationwide egg recall*. Retrieved from http://www.fda.gov/newsevents/newsroom/pressannouncements/ucm223248.htm

FDA. (2010b, October 18). *FDA authorizes Hillandale Farms to begin shipping fresh shell eggs*. Retrieved from http://www.fda.gov/NewsEvents/Newsroom/PressAnnouncements/ucm230041.htm

FDA. (2010c, October 18). *FDA issues warning letter to Wright County Egg*. Retrieved from http://www.fda.gov/NewsEvents/Newsroom/PressAnnouncements/ucm230051.htm

FDA. (2010 d, October 18). *Recall of shell eggs*. Retrieved from http://www.fda.gov/Safety/Recalls/MajorProductRecalls/ucm223522.htm

Glik, D. C. (2007). Risk communication for public health emergencies. *Annual Review of Public Health, 28*, 33–54.

Harris, G. (2010, September 22). *Egg producer says his business grew too quickly*. Retrieved from http://www.nytimes.com/2010/09/23/business/23eggs.html

Heath, R. L., & O'Hair, H. D. (Eds.). (2010). *Handbook of risk and crisis communication*. New York: Routledge.

Hillandale Farms. (2010, August 20). *Hillandale Farms (egg recall information)*. Retrieved from http://www.hillandalefarms.com/Recall.htm

Iannelli, V. (2010, December 1). *Egg recall timeline*. Retrieved from http://pediatrics.about.com/od/recallsandsafetyalerts/a/2010_egg_recall_2.htm

Jalonick, M. C. (2010, August 22). *Egg recall: Supplier Austin "Jack" Decoster has history of health, safety violations*. Retrieved from http://www.huffingtonpost.com/2010/08/22/egg-recall-supplier-violations_n_690400.html

Kutner, M., Greenberg, E., Jin, Y., & Paulsen, C. (2006). *The health literacy of America's adults: Results from the 2003 National Assessment of Adult Literacy* (NCES 2006–483).U.S. Department of Education.Washington, DC: National Center for Education Statistics.

Lewis, B., & Lewis, J. (2015). *Health communication: A media and cultural studies approach*. New York: Palgrave Macmillan.

Littlefield, R. S., Farrell, L., Beauchamp, K., & Rathnasinghe, S. (2012, November). Maintaining relationships with the public: Applications of relational dialectics theory in crisis situations. Paper presented at National Communication Association Conference, Orlando, FL.

National Network of Libraries of Medicine. (2010, September 14). *Health literacy*. Retrieved from http://nnlm.gov/outreach/consumer/hlthlit.html

Pew Research Center. (2010). Retrieved from www.pewresearch.org

Quality Eggs LLC. (2010, August 27). *A message about safe Maine eggs*. Retrieved from http://www.qualityegg.net/message-to-maine-consumers.html

Seeger, M. W. (2006). Best practices in crisis communication: An expert panel process. *Journal of Applied Communication Research, 34*(3), 232–244. doi: 10.1080/00909880600769944

Sellnow, D., & Mountford, R. (2011). *Oral and written communication*. Mason, OH: Cengage Learning.

Sellnow, T. L., Ulmer, R. R., Seeger, M. W. & Littlefield, R. (2009). *Effective risk communication: A message-centered approach*. New York: Springer Science + Business Media, LLC.

Sellnow, T. L., & Vidoloff, K. G. (2009). Getting crisis communication right. *Food Technology, 63*(9), 40–45.

Sellnow, T. L., Wickline, M., & Veil, S. R. (2013). Responding effectively to crises: Best practices in organizational crisis communication. In J. S. Wrench (Ed.), *Workplace communication for the 21st Century* (235–252). Santa Barbara, CA: ABC-CLIO.

Veil, S. R., & Husted, R. A. (2012). Best practices as an assessment for crisis communication. *Journal of Communication Management, 16*(2), 131–145.

Chapter Nine

Reflecting on Dialectical Tensions in Risk and Crisis Communication

Lessons Learned and Future Opportunities

Timothy L. Sellnow

Prior to Seeger's (2006) article, now one of the most referenced articles ever published in the *Journal of Applied Communication Research,* much of the work professing the best practices of crisis communication was anecdotal. Practitioners proclaimed their personal lists of "do's and don'ts" based on what had worked for them in the past. Limited attention was paid to audience complexity or the rapidly changing communication landscape. Seeger's essay was based on research grounded in the work and recommendations of those in the academy who studied crisis communication empirically. He also challenged scholars to engage in research to test, validate, negate, amend, and extend the best practices. This book has embraced that challenge by introducing dialectical tensions to the discussion and debate over what constitutes best practices for crisis communication.

Although the study of dialectical tensions typically is initiated from an interpersonal communication perspective, Littlefield and the contributing authors have shown the viability of the conceptual framework to function in an organizational setting. As the cases reveal, the spokespersons for the organizations studied in this volume faced tensions in their contemplation of how and when to respond to crises. Each of the case studies identified a vivid tension that was central to an organization's crisis message. In some cases, the tensions influenced the form and function of the messages shared. In other cases, the tension inspired a degree of reticence that limited the organization's ability to meet the needs of their vulnerable publics. In both circumstances, Seeger's (2006) best practices, including a failure to meet them, are at play.

As Littlefield argued in the introduction, dialectical tensions in risk and crisis communication are not inherently a sign weakness or failure. Rather, the tensions are a manifestation of the organization's relationships with its publics. The publics' desire for both the information that is known and the information that is unknown combine to create a communication context where tensions naturally emerge for organizational decision-makers and spokespersons. In addition, regulatory agencies, industry leaders, watchdog organizations, and other rivals contribute to the sea of information during a crisis. Littlefield explained that these multiple voices actually compete for the publics' attention. Thus, organizations must communicate effectively if they have any hope of influencing the narrative related to the crises they face. When we view crises from the perspective of dialectical tensions, we acknowledge the fact that "meaning comes from expression of competing voices" (introduction). The dialectical tensions framework reveals the importance of attending to rather than silencing these competing voices.

The chapters in this book teach valuable lessons about risk and crisis communication and planning. Each author identified multiple voices and the resulting tensions emerging in some of the nation's most compelling food-related crises over the past decade. Clearly, these lessons inform our understanding of best practices for risk and crisis communication. In the following section, I summarize what I believe are some of the key lessons revealed by the authors' application of dialectical tensions and best practices to the cases analyzed.

LESSONS LEARNED FROM DIALECTICAL TENSIONS

Seeger (2006) did not propose the best practices as a static summary of the field. Rather, he provided a clear statement of the best practices, as observed at that time, and invited scholars to test, confirm, question, and expand them. This book has contributed to that process. The analysis has shown how the best practices function from a perspective of multiple, often competing voices. Specifically, the dialectical tensions framework offers lessons related to audience analysis, the need for a situational focus, paradoxical demands of openness, failures in sensitivity, and attending to multiple voices. I discuss each of these lessons in the following paragraphs.

Audience Analysis

Perhaps most importantly, a focus on dialectical tensions demands audience awareness and analysis. If, after all, an organization perceives communication tensions arising during a crisis, that organization must recognize with whom the tensions exist. This recognition defies the temptation by organizations to engage in a purely linear or unidirectional distribution rather than exchange of information during a crisis. Even if organizations choose to withhold information, they do so with the conscious awareness that they are violating audience expectations. Ideally, recognizing dialectical tensions can inspire an organization to enact those best practices that resolve or diminish the tension. Either way, observing and responding to tensions engages the leaders of organizations in the active consideration of their audiences and the expectations of those audiences. The perspective of dialectical tensions provides a means for better understanding the influence of audiences on the decisions organizations make when responding to crises.

Roberts and Veil (chapter 8) used dialectical tensions to emphasize the need for organizations to engage in audience analysis during crises. They provided a detailed assessment of how both the media and egg producers failed to accurately analyze the needs of their audiences. The egg producers were concerned primarily with ensuing litigation. The media emphasized the breadth of the outbreak without clearly instructing consumers on how to protect themselves. Worried consumers were left with incomplete information at a time when a major portion of the country was susceptible to harm. In this case, the dialectical tension framework teaches valuable lessons about the role of audience and the need for audience analysis in crisis planning and communication.

Situational Focus

Government agencies such as the Centers for Disease Control and Prevention and the Department of Homeland Security have supported the exploration of an all-hazards approach to crisis communication (Sellnow & Seeger, 2013). The potential merit to this approach is obvious. If we understand the one best way to respond to crises, we can increase our efficiency in planning, coordination among agencies, and resource allocation. The risk of this approach is that we will miss the subtle nuances of crises as they unfold. The dialectical tensions framework exposes these subtleties and invites scholars to consider how organizations can best respond. This is not to say that best practices are unnecessary. Instead, the chapters in this book reveal the importance of recognizing and responding to the unusual aspects of each crisis.

Rick and Littlefield (chapter 6) revealed the situational constraints smaller organizations such as Del Bueno faced in responding to crises. Simply put, Del Bueno did not have the resources necessary to engage fully in the best practices for crisis communication. The company's leadership was open and honest, but could not overcome the problems with Listeria in its production facility. Ultimately, the situational constraints overwhelmed the company, and it was forced to permanently close all operations. Crisis planners and spokespersons stand to benefit from recognizing and responding to the unique or unusual tensions each crisis presents.

Paradox of Openness

Uncertainty is an inherent element of crises, yet stakeholders expect organizations and agencies to respond accurately and immediately from the first stages of a crisis. Simply put, crisis communicators face a paradoxical situation where they are expected to communicate with certainty in highly uncertain times. As Seeger (2006) explained in the best practices, crisis communicators should avoid the temptation to communicate with greater certainty than is warranted by the circumstances. Instead spokespersons should accept uncertainty by explaining what they know for certain, admitting what they do not know, and explaining what they are doing to gather more information.

The dialectical tensions perspective acknowledges the strain created by the paradoxical demands related to uncertainty. Haarstad and Littlefield (chapter 4) captured the perils of uncertainty in his assessment of the German *E. coli* outbreak. This case is remarkable in its complexity. Multiple nations, government agencies, and food products were intertwined in a terrifying crisis. Understandably, Europeans demanded certainty in recommendation from their governments on how to avoid consuming the deadly *E. coli.* strain. Spokespersons were pressured to make statements extending beyond their level of certainty. As a result, long-term damage was done to producers and international relationships. The dialectical tensions perspective revealed the multiple points of conflict simultaneously occurring in this crisis. In so doing, the conceptual framework of dialectical tensions expands our comprehension of the many forms of conflict that are caused by and intensified by the paradox of uncertainty.

Failures in Sensitivity

The dialectical tensions framework invites communicators to monitor their communication and to display sensitivity to the evolving perceptions and emotional needs of others. This need for sensitivity is, at least metaphorically, expressed at the organizational level in the cases reviewed for this book. Organizations may respond to a crisis with a communication strategy that serves their immediate needs, but lacks sensitivity to other stakeholders. Further, a communication strategy that seems appropriate at one stage of the crisis may lack sensitivity at other stages.

Peanut Corporation of America (PCA) and Menu Foods are two compelling examples of organizational insensitivity. PCA was sluggish in responding publicly to its crisis and eventually chose to disengage from consumers. Rathnasinghe and Littlefield (chapter 2) explained that Internet access and social media have intensified the expectation by consumers that information will be released rapidly as a crisis unfolds. These expectations intensified public outrage against PCA. Rathnasinghe and Littlefield found that PCA lacked a crisis management plan. This absence of planning, along with questionable practices, contributed to insensitivity toward the company's audience. In contrast, Menu Foods realized the severity of the crisis it faced, but experienced a disconnection with its audience. Farrell (chapter 3) observed that Menu Foods perceived itself as a victim in the melamine crisis. Although this perception was accurate to some degree, Farrell argued that it offered little solace to pet owners. As a result, Menu Foods was seen as insensitive. The conceptual framework of dialectical tensions offers a warning against such insensitivity in crisis situations.

Multiple Voices

As Littlefield articulated at the outset of this book, the dialectical tensions perspective emphasizes the process in which meaning is derived through competing voices. Whether the voice from one perspective is ultimately deemed accurate or inaccurate is less important than the contribution that voice makes to the larger discussion. The notion of competing voices is clearly relevant to the study of crisis communication. Recent publications on the status of the field of risk and crisis communication research, such as the *Handbook of Risk and Crisis Communication* (Heath & O'Hair, 2010) and the *Handbook of Crisis Communication* (Coombs & Holladay, 2010), have emphasized the need for scholars to move beyond the organizations facing crises and account for the multiple stakeholders impacted by crises. As the chapters in this book clearly indicated, the dialectical tensions framework offers a means for meeting this challenge.

Freed and Littlefield's (chapter 6) analysis of the melamine in milk crisis displayed the capacity for the dialectical tensions framework to account for multiple voices. The Chinese government, Sanlu, the New Zealand government, and twenty-two other companies in China all responded to the crisis. Combined, their voices influenced the development of policies worldwide aimed at curbing economic adulteration in the food supply. Similarly, the PCA case analyzed by Rathnasinghe and Littlefield (chapter 2) impacted literally hundreds of other organizations that had used PCA ingredients in their products. Eventually, the FDA and CDC emerged as credible information sources consumers could consult as new products were recalled daily. These crises revealed that monitoring a single voice or even a single tension through a crisis yields a very limited understanding. Conversely, a much more comprehensive view of multiple and competing voices reveals the true nature of a crisis.

DIALECTICAL TENSIONS AND THE EVOLUTION OF THE BEST PRACTICES

As discussed above, the application of dialectical tensions to recent crisis events in the food industry revealed considerable potential or further expanding and clarifying the best practices. For example, the notion of timeliness has been studied primarily from the perspective of a single organization or government agency sharing information publicly without intentional delay. Dialectical tensions research introduces the possibility that timeliness can mean drastically different things to different parties. While PCA intentionally avoided or delayed communicating publicly, the German government's anxiousness to communicate publicly was problematic. Similarly, expectations for being open and honest are influenced by the perspective an organization takes. For example, Menu Foods communicated in an open and honest manner from its perspective as a victim of the crisis. This perspective, however, did not mesh well with the needs of consumers.

The German *E. coli* crisis also extends the best practice of accepting uncertainty. Few would argue with the need to accept uncertainty during crises. The German *E. coli* outbreak, however, revealed that the expectations for admitting uncertainty differed widely among consumers, food producers, and government agencies. The Sanlu and Del Bueno crises further emphasized the tensions related to culture and how these tensions influence an organization's capacity to cooperate fully with regulatory agencies.

Petrun's analysis of Proposition 37 foods (chapter 7) emphasized variance that develops when two compelling narratives compete for acceptance. Those in favor of Proposition 37 threatened to discredit the FDA and the abundance of scientific evidence upon which the agency based its opinion. Proposition 37 is an example of how the tension created by multiple spokespersons espousing contradictory can threaten an organization's credibility and reputation. Similarly, Haarstad and Littlefield's assessment of the German *E. coli* case revealed a situation where multiple organizations and governments communicated simultaneously to diverse and highly alarmed sets of stakeholders. As Haarstad and Littlefield noted, these multiple spokespersons created confusion and frustration for a fearful audience. These cases and the dialectical tensions perspective raise questions about how to best acknowledge public concern.

Roberts and Veil, in their assessment of the massive egg recall, revealed tensions that emerge when organizations and agencies seek to cooperate with the media to share information rapidly with the public. Their finding that the great majority of the media's messages lacked essential information for self-protection is troubling. The case revealed a disconnection between the media's reporting and the priorities expressed by government agencies concerned with public health. This case draws attention to the need for further research and collaboration if crisis communicators are to fully engage in a collaboration with the media.

These are a few examples of how the dialectical tensions framework offers refreshing insight into the best practices summarized by Seeger (2006). The inclusive view of multiple parties and their messages afforded by the dialectical tensions framework has considerable potential for expanding and clarifying the best practices. Clearly, future research from this perspective is warranted.

EVOLVING TENSIONS IN A GLOBAL SOCIETY

Three decades ago, Perrow (1984) warned of an increasing closeness or tight coupling between industry and society. Such tight coupling, he warned, removes the cushion between industrial catastrophes and residents. As a result, a crisis that would have only injured workers and a limited number of residents now has the potential to harm thousands. The rise in technology and the globalization of the world's economy has created another form of tight coupling. In modern society, a nuclear accident in Japan has an impact on citizens an ocean away. The economic decline of one region profoundly impacts regions on the other side of the globe. The dialectical tensions framework offers a means for comprehending the impact of this increasing interdependence or tight coupling. Discussions of technical advances have moved from a community, country, or region to a worldwide debate. Questions over climate change and genetically modified organisms, for example, are also now issues of worldwide debate.

Advances in social media also influence the quantity and quality of relationships and information exchange surrounding risk and crisis communication. Voices previously silenced by government censorship now resonate through social media. Ding (2009) argued that social media access has allowed some citizens to overcome government restrictions using what he calls "guerrilla media" tactics to form virtual interpersonal relationships (p. 330). These relationships were prevalent in China during the SARS outbreak of 2003. Individuals used guerilla media tactics to acquire and share information that contested the information shared by the government media in China. Clearly, this defiant application of social media opens an entirely new set of dialectical tensions for consideration in crisis situations.

The virtual communities Ding (2009) observed are evolving in diversity and complexity. Individuals from different continents can align in support of common causes, creating dialectical tensions in a form and frequency beyond what has existed in the past. Seemingly disparate voices now interact through virtual communities that Falkheimer and Heide (2009) likened to "great good places" (p. 62). Great good places of the past included locations such as community cafes, barbershops or hair salons, and parks. Although these locations are still options, many individuals establish interpersonal relationships through virtual communities. When crises strike, virtual communities play a vital role in accessing and analyzing information. In some cases, the crisis itself initiates the creation of virtual communities. The communication exchanged through these virtual communities is certainly susceptible to the same general forms of dialectical tensions caused by face-to-face interaction or exposure to traditional media.

The chapters in this book have anticipated the shifting landscape of risk and crisis communication. Each chapter considered culture as a potential variable in the development and resolution of dialectical tensions. All but one of the cases analyzed in the book involved interactions among multiple countries, and all of the case analyses revealed tensions that, to varying degrees, had impacts that were intensified for underrepresented populations. Culture has always been an important factor in crisis communication. As our world continues to evolve toward a more globalized society, increased attention on the impact of culture in crisis communication is essential.

CONCLUSION AND IMPLICATIONS

This book has established the viability of dialectical tensions as a means for comprehending the successes and failures of crisis communicators. The perspective has merit for crisis planning, developing messages during crises, and for learning from crisis events. Organizations can inform their planning procedures by anticipating the tensions they might face with the various segments of their complex audience. During crises, spokespersons can recognize the tensions that emerge, accept that they exist, and address them. The case studies provided in this book offer vivid evidence that ignoring or looking beyond such tensions diminishes the quality of an organization or agency's crisis response. Finally, organizations can add dialectical tensions to their post-crisis learning. Were there tensions that should have been anticipated, but were not? Were there tensions that could not be resolved? Were some tensions resolved effectively? These are questions that can help an organization or agency learn from a crisis.

The cases in this book also revealed that our understanding of the best practices for crisis communication is enhanced when we consider their function and effectiveness from novel perspectives. Much of the research to date on crisis communication has relied on perspectives from organizational communication, public relations, argumentation, and rhetoric. Although dialectical tensions are usually considered on an interpersonal level, the cases provided in this book exemplify the perspective's adaptability. Specifically, dialectical tensions enable a focus on audience complexity and cultural sensitivity that extends beyond theories previously applied to such crises. Future research will benefit from taking such novel perspectives in assessing the best practices of risk and crisis communication. As such, this book serves as an invitation to crisis communication scholars to embrace new perspectives.

REFERENCES

Coombs, W. T., & Holladay, J. S. (Eds.). (2010). *The handbook of crisis communication.* Malden, MA: Wiley Blackwell.

Ding, H. (2009). Rhetorics of alternative media in an emerging epidemic: Censorship, and extra-institutional risk communication. *Technical Communication Quarterly, 18*(4), 327–350. doi: 10.10.1080/10572250903149548

Falkheimer, J., & Heide, M., (2009). Crisis communication in a new world: Reaching multicultural publics through old and new media. *Nordicom Review, 30,* 55–65.

Heath, R. L., & O'Hair, H. D. (Eds.). (2010). *Handbook of risk and crisis communication.* New York: Routledge.

Perrow, C. (1984). *Normal accidents.* New York: Basic Books.

Seeger, M. W. (2006). Best practices in crisis communication: An expert panel process *Journal of Applied communication Research, 34,* 232–244.

Sellnow, T. L. & Seeger, M. W. (2013). *Theorizing crisis communication.* Malden, MA: Wiley Blackwell.

Index